BREAKTHROUGH!

BREAK

THROUGH!

How Three People Saved
"BLUE BABIES"
and Changed Medicine Forever

JIM MURPHY

CLARION BOOKS

Houghton Mifflin Harcourt

Boston   New York

Clarion Books

215 Park Avenue South

New York, New York 10003

Clarion Books is an imprint of Houghton Mifflin Harcourt Publishing Company.

www.hmhco.com

The text was set in Legacy Serif.

Library of Congress Cataloging-in-Publication Data

Murphy, Jim, 1947–

Breakthrough! : how three people saved "blue babies" and changed medicine forever / Jim Murphy.

pages cm

Audience: Age 9–12.

Summary: "The story of the landmark 1944 surgical procedure that repaired the heart of a child with blue baby syndrome—lack of blood oxygen caused by a congenital defect. The team that developed the procedure included a cardiologist and a surgeon, but most of the actual work was done by Vivien Thomas, an African American lab assistant who was frequently mistaken for a janitor"—Provided by publisher.

ISBN 978-0-547-82183-2 (hardback)

1. Thomas, Vivien T., 1910-1985—Juvenile literature. 2. Blalock, Alfred, 1899–1964—Juvenile literature. 3. Taussig, Helen B. (Helen Brooke), 1898-1986—Juvenile literature. 4. Surgeons—Maryland—Biography—Juvenile literature. 5. Cardiovascular system—Surgery—Juvenile literature. 6. Heart—Surgery—Juvenile literature. I. Title.

RD27.35.T46M87 2015

617'.0232—dc23

2015013601

Manufactured in China

SCP 10 9 8 7 6 5 4 3 2 1

4500544781

To my childhood physician, Dr. George F. Simms, who traveled to his first patients via horse and buggy and was still practicing medicine seven decades later,

and

To my present GP, Dr. Michael A. Parziale, who is highly knowledgeable and informative and does his work with easy grace and humor

There are men and women, but not a great number, created for the service of Medicine: who were called to be doctors when they were not yet called to be babies.

Dr. Stephen Paget, 1908

CONTENTS

PREFACE   xi

ONE: In the "Dog House"   1

TWO: The Professor and His Assistant   16

THREE: Surrounded by Failure   27

FOUR: Answered and Unanswered Questions   37

FIVE: The Search   47

SIX: "All the World Is Against It"   55

SEVEN: "Vivien, You'd Better Come Down Here"   66

EIGHT: Then What Happened?   75

ACKNOWLEDGMENTS   101

SOURCE NOTES   103

BIBLIOGRAPHY   121

PICTURE CREDITS   123

INDEX   125

PREFACE

THE cast-iron radiator in Johns Hopkins Hospital operating room 706 rattled and hissed but didn't give off much heat on the morning of November 29, 1944. Outside, a miserable, cold rain was falling, allowing only a feeble bit of gray light to seep through the room's large windows.

The somber atmosphere was matched by the mood of the surgeon, Dr. Alfred Blalock, and the seven other people who made up his surgical team. And for good reason. The patient they were about to operate on, Eileen Saxon, was eighteen months old and weighed only 8.8 pounds. Eileen had a severe congenital heart defect that made it difficult for her to breathe and turned the skin on parts of her body an unhealthy-looking dark color. Dr. William Longmire, assisting Blalock that morning, was absolutely horrified by what he saw. "I took one look at the little patient and thought, 'My God, this man isn't going to operate on her!' I thought that after [the initial] incision . . . this child would surely die."

Others had worried that simply administering the anesthetic might kill Eileen. Dr. Austin Lamont, the chief of anesthesia at Johns Hopkins, felt the girl's health was so fragile that he refused to assist Blalock.

No doctor who examined the girl would have disagreed with Lamont's assessment. Eileen was gravely ill and about to die. But Blalock and the head of the Children's Cardiac Clinic, Dr. Helen Taussig, had argued that it was precisely because she was so close to death that the surgery was necessary. Eileen's condition was rapidly deteriorating, they explained. She might live for a few hours, possibly even a day, but probably not much longer. The operation, if successful, was the only way to prolong her life.

The procedure was allowed to go forward, but the words "if successful" haunted Blalock. Responsibility for the operation and for Eileen's life rested squarely on his shoulders. Self-doubt had been nagging at him since he'd first scheduled the surgery a few days before. At one point, he grew so upset over some research experiments that hadn't gone well that he blurted out to Longmire, "Bill, I am discouraged. Nothing I do seems to work these days." His lack of confidence had been following him everywhere and at all times. The night before the procedure Blalock had a difficult time sleeping; the next morning he was so distracted and nervous that he decided he couldn't drive safely and asked his wife to drive him to the hospital.

It wasn't only that the operation was very complex and risky. The surgery he was about to perform on Eileen's struggling heart had never been done on a human before, let alone one so tiny or frail. This was why the balcony-type observation stand along the west side of room 706 was packed with curious Johns Hopkins staff and why a movie camera had been set up pointing at the operating table. If the operation worked—if the patient survived—history would be made.

Moreover, Blalock had never performed this procedure, not even on an experimental animal. In fact, the only person to have done it successfully, start to finish, wasn't an official member of the surgical team. According to hospital rules, he wasn't even supposed to be in the room. But he was there now, at Blalock's request, standing just behind the surgeon on a wooden step stool. His name was Vivien Thomas, and most people at the hospital thought he was a janitor.

CHAPTER ONE

In the "Dog House"

VIVIEN Thomas took one look at the old Hunterian Laboratory on the Johns Hopkins campus and his heart sank. The building was squat and dour looking, an unruly growth of vines barely covering an undistinguished brick exterior. The interior was no better. The walls were painted a "drab hospital-green," Thomas remembered, and "[Dr. Blalock and I] were greeted by the odor from the [experimental] animal quarters in the basement. No wonder people referred to the building as the 'dog house.'"

Thomas had mixed emotions about following Blalock to Johns Hopkins University as his research assistant in 1941. The city of Baltimore was teeming with activity because the United States would very soon be at war with Germany and Japan. In addition to being a major seaport, Baltimore was a center of shipbuilding and steel production, both important industries during wartime. "Baltimore was one of the busiest cities in the country,"

Vivien Thomas with his wife, Clara, and their daughters, 1941.

Thomas noted. "Jobs were plentiful and people were coming from all over the country to fill them." The arrival of thousands of workers and their families had resulted in a severe housing shortage.

Thomas and his wife, Clara, had grown up in "individual

dwellings with lawns and trees that allowed for some outdoor living—what I called a little elbow room." The Thomases were unable to find such a place in Baltimore. Rental houses of this type were unavailable, not just because the recent influx of workers had made housing scarce, but because Thomas and his wife were African American. Real estate agents simply refused to show them houses in all-white suburbs.

Racial prejudice and segregation weren't new experiences for Thomas and his wife. They had always lived in the South, first in a moderate-sized Louisiana town near the Gulf of Mexico, then in the larger city of Nashville, Tennessee. Both states had oppressive Jim Crow laws on the books, statutes that kept African American citizens separate from their white counterparts. Public bathrooms, restaurants, trolley cars, schools, hospitals, cemeteries, swimming pools, drinking fountains, prisons, and even churches existed for whites and blacks, but never for both together. Even with these unfair restrictions in place, Thomas had always been able to rent a real house with a yard. Until, that is, he got to Baltimore.

Thomas had been hoping that Baltimore, being farther north than any other city he'd lived in, would be somewhat more tolerant. Sadly, as the historian C. Fraser Smith points out, "There was little difference from the deep south. There were just as many exclusions for black people in Baltimore as anyplace else." A glance

When Thomas moved to Baltimore, the city was strictly segregated. Most amenities and facilities were clearly marked for who was allowed to use them. Even buying a soda from the wrong machine could lead to arrest or violence.

around Johns Hopkins would have told Thomas this: every bathroom was clearly marked either WHITE or COLORED.

Frustrated and annoyed, Thomas was forced to search for an apartment in the "congested, treeless, grassless" inner city. "Many of the apartments that bore 'for rent' signs could hardly be classified as fit for human habitation," Thomas complained. "I finally found an apartment which was really marginal as living quarters, but I decided to take it with the hope of finding something more suitable [at a later time]." It would take Thomas and his wife more than a year to find a larger, nicer apartment.

Now he and Blalock went up the stairs at the foul-smelling

The Hunterian Laboratory at Johns Hopkins, referred to as the "dog house" because it smelled so awful.

Hunterian Laboratory where they would work. Thomas found their spaces a dirty wreck, with peeling paint, old, rusty pipes, a thick layer of dust on countertops, broken glass and wadded pieces of paper on the floor.

Thomas nimbly slid his tall, thin body around the dirty tables, benches, and chairs. He ran his long index finger along the surface of a table, looked at the sooty dirt gathered on his fingertip, and shook his head in disgust. There was no excuse for such neglect and filth, especially in a medical research laboratory.

After they discussed the dilapidated condition of the

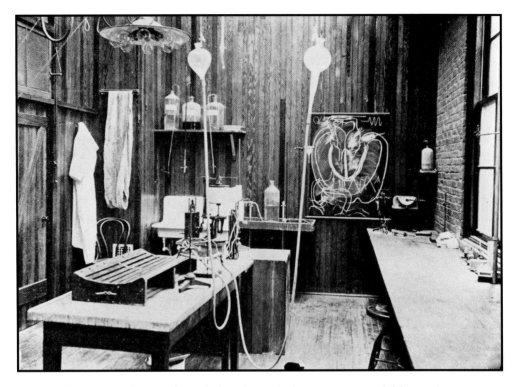

There was nothing modern, sleek, or hygienic about most research laboratories when Blalock and Thomas started at Johns Hopkins.

laboratory and office, Blalock asked Thomas to clean up the space and paint the large classroom-laboratory and two smaller adjacent rooms a lively color. Having already worked for Blalock at Vanderbilt Medical School in Nashville for more than eleven years, the thirty-one-year-old Thomas had long ago outgrown this sort of menial job. But, he recalled, "I would have agreed to almost anything to change what, to me, was a depressing and almost revolting atmosphere. If he had suggested tearing the building down and erecting a new one, I would have gladly accepted the challenge."

Thomas set to work during the steamy hot months of July and August, painting the walls, cleaning and waxing the grimy floors, washing windows, piling trash in the garbage can—doing anything he could to spruce up the lab. He was also trying to assemble up-to-date equipment so that he and Blalock could resume their research.

While he was ordering two vital items for experimental surgery, Thomas encountered the same prejudice he had met while house hunting. To get new equipment, Thomas had to submit requests to the director of the laboratory, Dr. Edgar Poth. Poth was extremely civil to Thomas, but he refused to order the items requested. When Thomas tried to explain why he and Dr. Blalock needed the equipment, Poth cut him off sharply and pointedly told him that he would have to make do with what was already available. Poth added that he did not want to discuss the matter with Thomas again.

"I did not feel it was incumbent upon me to try to force the issue," Thomas recalled, so "I had no alternative but to tell Dr. Blalock what I had been told."

Blalock had been champing at the bit for weeks to get his research projects up and running and was in no mood to hear about further delays. He usually spoke in a soft, gentlemanly manner, with a slight southern accent. But when Thomas told him what had happened, Blalock exploded. "Who the hell does he think he is?" he demanded. "I run this department. Tell him." He reached for a piece of paper and wrote in very bold longhand: "Dr. Poth — Get everything Vivien asks for for my work," and signed it. He turned to Thomas and said, "Here, give it to him."

For Blalock, this situation represented a simple if annoying turf battle. Poth was a part of the old guard at Johns Hopkins, people who wanted to continue to follow the easy and established ways and avoid any unnecessary and annoying change in their work routines. Blalock had been made head of the laboratory as well as head of surgery specifically to change such attitudes; his goal was not to maintain the status quo but to make the research facility one of the best in the country, if not the world.

Blalock's note put Thomas in an awkward, even dangerous, position. Thomas was new to the hospital, and was officially listed as a laboratory assistant. Because every other African American working at Johns Hopkins was a janitor, waiter, or cook, most people at the hospital thought Thomas was merely a janitor. Now he was in effect going to insist that a white doctor do something he had categorically refused to do.

Thomas had good reason to be concerned. At the time, a seemingly innocent interaction between a black person and a white person could go from civil to tense to violent very easily. Throughout the South, an African American had been hanged, burned alive, or beaten to death by a white mob every four days from 1889 through 1929. The alleged crimes of these victims included "frightening school children," "seeking employment in a restaurant," and "trying to act like a white man." At least sixty-six were murdered for "insult to a white person." And the violence continued into the 1930s and 1950s. In historian Isabel Wilkerson's words, "In everyday interactions, a black person could not contradict a white person or speak unless spoken to first. . . . The consequences for the slightest misstep were swift and brutal."

After an African American mother and her son were lynched for alleged crimes, the lynch mob lined up on the bridge to be photographed. Photos such as this were often printed as postcards and sent to friends as souvenirs.

Thomas was a tall, physically fit man and not at all afraid of confronting people he felt were wrong. At Johns Hopkins, for instance, Thomas ignored the WHITE signs on the bathrooms and used whichever one was nearby. And he had stood his ground with Blalock himself years before, when they were still at Vanderbilt University. Thomas had made an error while carrying out an experiment, and "Dr. Blalock sounded off like a child throwing a temper tantrum. The profanity he used would have made the proverbial sailor proud of him."

Thomas's response to this tongue-lashing spoke volumes about his character. After Blalock stormed from the room, Thomas calmly changed into his street clothes and went to Blalock's office, where he asked to be paid off. "I told him . . . if it was going to be like this every time I made a mistake, my staying around would only cause trouble. I said I had not been brought up to take or use the kind of language he had used across the hall."

Blalock's family were southern aristocracy and had been the owners of several plantations. His mother's people were directly related to Jefferson Davis, the president of the Confederacy during the Civil War. No one working for them, black or white, talked back.

Blalock was a proud product of that segregated past when both established laws and unspoken social rules created an invisible wall between whites and blacks. He grew up expecting to be listened to, not lectured. But Thomas's quiet dignity and his calm but determined manner impressed Blalock immensely. Besides, in the short period they had been working together, Blalock had come to respect and value Thomas's great skill and keen mind. Thomas recalled that after a brief pause, Blalock "apologized, saying that he had lost his temper, that he would watch his language, and asked me to go back to work."

When Thomas told a fellow employee what Blalock had said, the man laughed and predicted Blalock would probably yell at Thomas again, and soon. A half-century later, Thomas was able to say, "We had occasional disagreements and sometimes almost heated discussions. But Dr. Blalock kept his word for the next thirty-four years, even though I made mistakes."

Thomas was well aware that Poth might react in anger and that handing him the surgeon's note in person might cause serious trouble. Conflict with Poth might turn a great many people at the hospital against him and Dr. Blalock, which would undoubtedly slow down their research. Thomas wanted to avoid delays at all costs. So instead of delivering the note himself, he put it in an envelope and had Blalock's secretary leave it on Poth's desk.

As Thomas had anticipated, there were repercussions. "The day after the note was left on his desk, I greeted [Dr. Poth] in the

A thoughtful
Dr. Blalock studies a
patient's medical chart.

corridor, but my greeting was not acknowledged or returned. . . .
He never spoke to me [again], even though our [work spaces] were
next door to each other."

Not only did Thomas receive the silent treatment from
Poth, but he became aware that word about the Poth letter had
spread — or rather had been spread by prejudiced colleagues. This
probably surprised both Blalock and Thomas, but to many others it was business as usual. As C. Fraser Smith recalled, "[Johns]
Hopkins was regarded as prejudiced at the time. That was the
word that was used. That they were an implacable fortress."

Over the next week, Thomas and Blalock realized that their

newly painted and cleaned laboratory was beginning to look cluttered and dirty again. "Trash cans hadn't been emptied, the floor under the sink was piled high with used paper towels, the sink hadn't been cleaned, the floor hadn't been swept, the counter tops hadn't been wiped off or dusted."

Thomas investigated and discovered that the laboratory's white housekeeper "was taking care of the rest of the building, right up to our door. Why not our laboratory too?" Thomas, of course, had his suspicions: "Knowing Dr. Poth's attitude toward me, I believed he was orchestrating the entire situation."

Thomas had done the initial cleanup and painting to get the research projects moving forward again. But he had "no intention of cleaning here" on a regular basis. Once again, he went to Blalock, who sputtered and said, "Good Lord, I hope we aren't getting into trouble already!" Thomas's response was characteristically straightforward and practical: "I answered that we were going to have to face it now or later." There was a short period of complete silence; then Blalock jumped up, stood a moment next to his desk thinking, and left the laboratory at a brisk pace.

Blalock was not an imposing man physically, and his manner was that of a quiet, thoughtful person who didn't rock the boat; if anything, he came across as agreeable and passive. His privileged upbringing had given him a sense of his place in the world and an understanding of how to deal with people who dismissed his reasonable requests. But when Blalock went to confront another white man over the treatment of his black assistant, he was taking a risk, as Thomas had. He could find himself ostracized by colleagues at Johns Hopkins even before he had a chance to establish himself as a leader. As Blalock disappeared down the hall, Thomas "had a feeling that something was going to happen."

Something did happen between Blalock and Poth, though exactly what is unclear. Blalock never told Thomas what he did or said, and he never wrote about it. Clearly he viewed the racial prejudice his assistant was being subjected to as disruptive and hurtful; he probably also worried that if other members of the lab followed Poth's lead, Thomas might become fed up enough to quit.

Whatever was said seems to have worked. In the days to follow, the lab was always clean and tidy, though the housekeeper refused to enter Thomas's work area when he was there. Instead, she did her work well before Thomas arrived in the morning. She left Johns Hopkins a few months later. A year after the incident, Poth took another position deeper in the South, where Jim Crow laws were still strictly enforced.

No one would consider Blalock a civil rights advocate. He was too much a part of the established South to completely escape its conventions and prejudices. He and Thomas often had a glass of whiskey in the lab after work when they sat down to talk over projects, but they never had a drink together in public. Nevertheless, the way he had interceded on Thomas's behalf put others at Johns Hopkins on notice: anything that stood in the way of Dr. Blalock's research would not be tolerated, even if that meant his white colleagues had to treat Thomas as an equal. And so the Blalock-Thomas laboratory opened, and research experiments began again with uncompromising energy.

CHAPTER TWO

The Professor and His Assistant

WHEN Alfred Blalock came to Johns Hopkins, he had already achieved international fame. While at Vanderbilt he had conducted groundbreaking experiments on the cause and cure of shock, and he planned to carry on that research at Johns Hopkins.

The shock he researched is different from the shock someone might feel at receiving bad news or being surprised at night by someone leaping out and shouting *Boo!* Shock is also the name for a medical condition that can occur after a severe physical injury, such as being in a car crash, being cut or burned or wounded in battle, or falling hard to the ground. When Blalock began his research on shock at Vanderbilt in 1925, its symptoms were well known: they included a thin, rapid heartbeat; a sudden drop in blood pressure; intense thirst; fatigue; and cool, clammy skin. Once shock set in, the symptoms almost always became worse, and frequently resulted in a heart attack or kidney failure, either of which could cause death.

Despite a great deal of medical knowledge about the symptoms and effects of shock, no one knew what caused it or how to reverse it. At the time, the generally accepted notion was that shock made the body produce a poisonous substance, though no one could verify this.

The thirty-one-year-old Blalock was five years into his study of shock when nineteen-year-old Thomas applied for a job at Vanderbilt in 1930. Blalock was trying to establish a scientific understanding of shock. To accomplish this, he had to produce shock in experimental animals and then analyze the data he gathered, such as changes in blood pressure or in the level of oxygen in the blood. In addition to pursuing this research, Blalock's responsibilities included instructing medical students, taking care of patients, and numerous administrative duties. All these tasks were very time-consuming, which meant his research lagged.

Because of his many obligations, Blalock decided he needed

Blalock was very happy when he arrived at Vanderbilt University in 1925.

someone to help him out. But he wanted more than just a skilled technician to assist him; he needed a partner. He explained this to Thomas during his initial job interview at Vanderbilt and told him exactly what sort of person he was looking to hire: "I want to carry on my research and laboratory work and I want someone [here] I can teach to do anything I can do and maybe do things I can't do." To be certain he was clear, Blalock added,

Blalock lecturing medical students about surgery.

"I want someone who can get to the point that he can do things on his own even though I may not be around."

Blalock decided to hire Thomas, finding him intelligent, well-spoken, and curious. Thomas had asked a great many smart questions during the interview. Most important, he did not seem overwhelmed by the idea of doing complex research experiments.

For Thomas, if there was a downside to the position, it was the salary. He made twenty dollars a week as a carpenter, while Vanderbilt was willing to pay him only twelve dollars a week, the rate for a newly hired janitor. Even so, he accepted the job, planning to stay a very short while. "To me the job was a stop-gap measure to get me through the cold winter months," he recalled.

Thomas was born in August 1910 to Mary and William Thomas. They were hard-working and loving parents who encouraged their five children to pay attention in school and discouraged idleness and foolish behavior. "Our parents," Thomas said with pride, "took time to let us know, in no uncertain terms, what was expected of us, and we made every effort to live up to their expectations."

Both parents were highly skilled in their professions. His mother was an "excellent seamstress" and made all of the clothes her family wore, from dresses and blouses to pants, shirts, and jackets. Decades later, her precise, intricate needlework was something Thomas recalled vividly and imitated while performing surgery. His father was a master carpenter and successful contractor who worked mainly in the northwest section of Nashville, where the majority of the African American community lived. His hard work and frugal nature enabled him to purchase a half acre of land and build his own home there before Thomas was five years old.

Thomas's parents knew that the way to a secure life was through a solid education and the acquisition of real, marketable skills. Thomas and his two older brothers got an early start working for their father: "My father took advantage of the propensity of boys to hammer on things and brought us up in his own trade of carpentry." Beginning when he was thirteen, Thomas would report immediately after school to whatever job his father had in progress. "So we [worked] from 3:00 to 5:30. . . . We also worked from 7 a.m. until noon on Saturdays."

Thomas could do more than hammer a nail into wood. Over the course of several years, he learned how to hang doors, install flooring, and do very complicated finishing woodwork, all to his father's exacting standards. "I . . . learned the lesson which I still remember and try to adhere to [in my medical research]: whatever you do, always do your best; otherwise it might show up to haunt and embarrass you." Thomas was so adept at carpentry work that

Policemen shout out to the crowd that the bank behind them has just closed its doors and gone out of business.

"my father had me working almost independently by the time I was sixteen years old."

Thomas was paid for his work, and he carefully saved his money in hopes of attending college and eventually going on to medical school. Being a doctor had long been his goal. He had grown up admiring a local African American doctor, not just for his intelligence and important skills, but also for the respect he was shown by everyone in the community. Thomas's desire to earn a medical degree drove him to study hard, and he was accepted by Tennessee State College in 1929. But before he set foot inside a classroom, the stock market collapsed and sent the United States into the Great Depression. Thomas watched helplessly as the bank that held his tuition money closed its doors for good and his savings disappeared—along with his hopes of going to college. At the same time, the need for carpenters dried up as well.

It was this terrible personal loss that sent Thomas to apply for the job at Vanderbilt University in 1930. He needed work desperately and asked a friend if he knew of any job leads. The friend said he'd heard that the research laboratory there was looking for an assistant. Thomas clearly impressed Blalock, because he was offered the job on the spot and began work the very next day. Blalock had no way of knowing during the interview that Vivien Thomas was the answer to his prayers.

The Professor, as most people in the lab referred to the thirty-one-year-old doctor, plunged his new assistant into important research projects immediately. That first morning, Blalock arrived early to personally teach Thomas the technique of weighing a research animal to determine how much anesthesia it would need, how to prepare it for surgery, and how to administer the painkiller. Then he explained what he intended to do, demon-

Thomas in the Vanderbilt University laboratory, 1931.

strated how the procedure was done, and showed Thomas how to record the findings. "Dr. Blalock believed in statistics," Thomas observed, "and insisted on large numbers of experiments . . . in order to have meaningful statistics from which he could judge and draw conclusions."

Over the following weeks and months, Blalock trained his new assistant in a wide variety of challenging procedures. Blalock also had other doctors in the lab teach Thomas valuable

Blalock discovered that administering whole blood or plasma to a shock victim could avert long-term and sometimes fatal reactions. Here a medic is giving blood to a soldier wounded in combat during World War II.

skills—how to perform various surgical procedures, do complicated chemical analysis, and operate and repair equipment. Thomas was being given what amounted to crash versions of postgraduate courses with material he might have encountered in many advanced medical programs.

"The volume of work each day was tremendous," Thomas recalled. "Besides having an experiment in progress, the chemical analyses from the previous day's experiment were being done."

But something else—something surprising and amazing—was happening. Despite the low pay and Dr. Blalock's occasional grumpiness, Thomas found himself caught up in the Professor's obvious passion for his research. "I did not realize that enthusiasm was contagious until I found that I didn't mind if I had to cancel some social activity" to complete the day's work, he recalled.

For more than fifteen years, at Vanderbilt and then at Johns Hopkins, Blalock and Thomas carried out experiments on shock. The work took on real urgency when Blalock and Thomas moved into Johns Hopkins in 1941, with the United States on the verge of entering World War II; soldiers wounded on the battlefield were often shock victims. With Thomas's assistance, Blalock was able to show that shock wasn't caused by some unrecognized toxic agent produced by the body but resulted from a rapid loss of blood. He also suggested that the infusion of whole blood or plasma could minimize shock or even prevent it from occurring.

As often happens with new theories, some scientists questioned Blalock's results, mainly because his conclusions about the cause and treatment of shock seemed too simple. But during the course of the war, his ideas were proven to be correct and probably saved hundreds of thousands, if not millions, of military and civilian lives.

Blalock's study of shock did not end with the publication

of his scientific papers on the subject during the late 1930s and 1940s. And at Vanderbilt and Johns Hopkins, Thomas continued to absorb information and to perfect his research and surgical skills.

It seemed as if the Blalock/Thomas work routine would continue on the same path forever. Then they met Dr. Helen B. Taussig.

CHAPTER THREE

Surrounded by Failure

IF you look at a cutaway illustration of an adult human heart, you will see that it is made up of four distinct chambers. Two of them (the right atrium and right ventricle) pump blood that has been depleted of oxygen to the lungs, where new oxygen is added. The other two (the left atrium and left ventricle) pump the now-oxygenated blood throughout the body. But the heart of a developing human fetus is an even more stunningly amazing and strange thing.

In fact, a few-days-old fetus has no heart at all. It has two primitive heart tubes. As the fetus grows, the tubes are pushed together, and by the twenty-first day they actually fuse to form what looks like an X. This primitive heart begins beating at day twenty-two, and starts to twist and bend into what we might recognize as the familiar heart shape.

Meanwhile, the interior of the heart is slowly changing as

well. Over the following months it will grow from a single chamber into a two-, then three-, and finally a four-chambered heart. An unborn fetus doesn't need a fully functioning heart because its mother is supplying it with oxygen and nutrients through the placenta. To ensure that it is pumping blood to the lungs and then throughout the body as efficiently as possible, the heart continues to develop even after the baby is born.

Unless, of course, it doesn't.

Sometimes the heart of an unborn baby doesn't develop

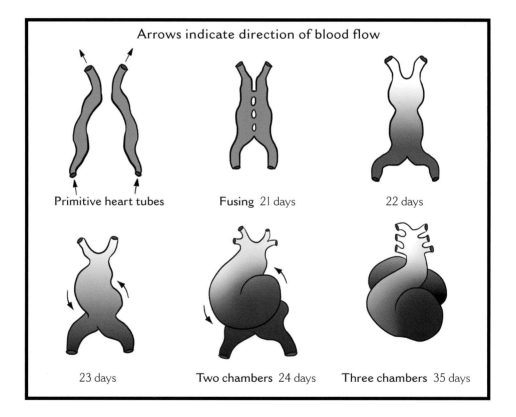

This sequence shows the development of the primitive heart tubes.

properly. "Congenital disease can warp the heart with great variety," says medical writer G. Wayne Miller. "Valves can be sealed tight, missing parts. . . . Major vessels can be misplaced, narrowed, or blocked completely. A chamber can be too small or missing, a wall too thick or thin. The muscle may be weak. Holes may occur almost anywhere, in almost any size."

Dr. Helen Taussig, the head of the Children's Cardiac Clinic at Johns Hopkins from 1930 to 1963, knew as much about heart defects in children as anyone in the world. She had more than two hundred malformed hearts floating in formaldehyde-filled glass jars at Johns Hopkins's pathology museum. They were there to be studied by Taussig and anyone else interested in abnormal hearts. They also represented something much more personal to Taussig. Each one had once beat in the chest of one of her patients; each one told her that aside from providing comfort and support and some basic medical assistance, such as oxygen, neither she nor anyone else had been able to help these patients and save their lives. She was, in fact, surrounded by failure: her own. But Helen Taussig was not the sort of person who gave up without a fight.

Taussig was born in Cambridge, Massachusetts, in 1898. She grew up tall and physically fit and was always either playing tennis, swimming, canoeing, or sailing. And she was extremely bright; before her mother became ill with tuberculosis, she taught Helen botany, while her father helped her learn German. Even with all of this positive experience, her childhood was plagued with adversity.

In elementary school, she barely passed arithmetic, and repeatedly failed in both reading and spelling. No matter how hard Taussig tried, she was unable to piece letters into words and read them. She had a learning disability known today as dyslexia. The situation worsened when at age thirteen she contracted a mild case of tuberculosis and could attend school only in the morning for over a year.

Taussig's mother had died when Helen was just eleven, so it was her father who sat with her day after day and patiently helped her with her studies, encouraging her to never give up on the task at hand or on herself. She would always have some difficulty reading, but with her father's guidance and her own strong will to learn, Taussig's grades gradually improved to the point where she wanted to attend medical school. "My father helped me to express myself clearly," Taussig would recall years later. She, like Thomas, was struggling to achieve her dreams against what must have seemed like insurmountable odds. And, like Thomas, her upbringing helped her in this battle. "[My father] also helped me to realize the importance of carrying through to completion any project I undertook."

Persevering despite obstacles would help Taussig obtain her medical degree and choose a specialty. Medicine was a white

Frank William Taussig appears stern, but his thoughtful, caring attention to his daughter's education helped her overcome many obstacles.

male-dominated profession when Taussig sought entrance to medical school in 1921. At that time, only 5 percent of practicing physicians in the United States were women. Most medical schools either barred women entirely or refused to grant them degrees even if they fulfilled all of the school's requirements. In other words, women were permitted to study medicine but not to practice medicine.

Taussig applied to Harvard Medical School and was admitted—but was allowed to take only a course or two at a time. She was the only female in her class and was made to sit apart from male students. When they studied microscope slides in the laboratory, Taussig had to sit by herself in another room "so I wouldn't contaminate the other—male—students!"

Fortunately, a professor in one of her Harvard classes noticed her ability and recommended that she study at Boston University, where she could take a full range of courses for credit. While she was at BU, another professor, Dr. Alexander Begg, suggested she might want to specialize in conditions of the heart, and after she demonstrated great skill in her studies, he helped her apply to Johns Hopkins Medical School to earn her medical degree.

She must have impressed her teachers there, because when the pediatric cardiac clinic was set up in 1930, the thirty-two-year-old Taussig was asked to run it. Taussig's professional career was definitely on the rise when she faced another serious challenge: she began to lose her hearing.

No one would ever be able to tell her why this happened, though one doctor speculated that it might have been the result of a bout of whooping cough. Whatever the cause, impaired hearing made listening to a child's heartbeat very difficult and put her medical career in jeopardy.

After her initial panic subsided, Taussig did what came naturally to her — she looked for ways to solve the problem. When her first hearing aid turned out to be insufficient, she taught herself how to read lips and bought a special stethoscope that amplified sound.

Finally, Taussig taught herself the unique skill of "listening" with her fingers when examining a young patient. She did this by gently holding the tips of her fingers against a child's chest so she

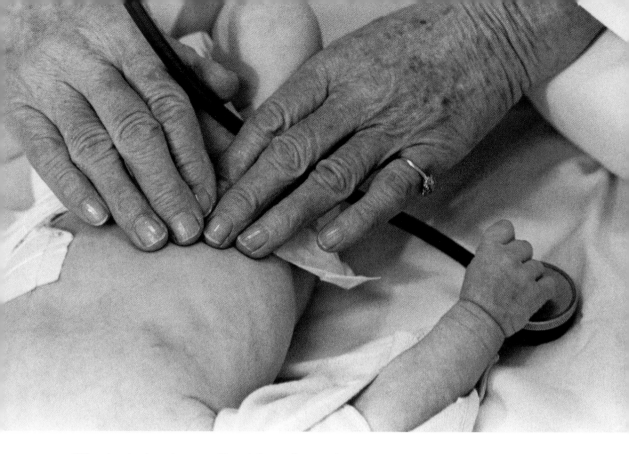

When hearing loss threatened her ability to diagnose her young patients, Helen Taussig developed a way to "listen" to a tiny beating heart with her fingertips.

could feel the heart's pulsations and gather other medical information. "Adversity," medical historian Joyce Baldwin concluded, "was an excellent teacher to Helen. It deepened her compassion for others and taught her the value of persevering. . . . Gentleness was her hallmark in treating patients, who immediately sensed this quality in her and felt safe with her."

But perseverance and gentleness weren't saving her patients' lives. This was especially true of babies born with a heart defect called tetralogy of Fallot, better known as "blue baby syndrome."

Even though researchers before him had studied and described tetralogy of Fallot, research conducted by the French physician Étienne-Louis Arthur Fallot in 1888 was so admired by colleagues that the condition was named for him.

During his career, Dr. Robert Gross developed many innovative techniques to save children with congenital heart defects, but he dismissed Taussig's idea of supplying additional oxygen to damaged hearts through surgery.

A child with this condition is born with four separate and very serious malformations of the heart, all of which result in insufficient oxygen in the blood being circulated through the body. Oxygen-rich blood is bright red; deoxygenated blood is blue, and this color can be seen where blood is close to the surface of the skin (such as near the lips, toes, and fingertips).

The bluish skin tone wasn't the major problem these children faced. Twenty-five percent of children born with tetralogy of Fallot died before their first birthday; 70 percent were dead by the age of ten. Taussig felt that the lack of oxygen in the bloodstream weakened these infants and strained their heart so much that in time their heart simply failed.

In 1938, Taussig saw a glimmer of hope. That year Harvard surgeon Robert E. Gross successfully repaired a common birth defect of the heart called patent ductus arteriosus. Normally, the patent ductus vessel closes on its own shortly after birth so that the aorta and the pulmonary artery are separated. In patent ductus arteriosus they remain connected, allowing too much oxygen-rich blood to mix with oxygen-poor blood. The two supplies of blood create an excess of fluid that puts a great strain on the heart and can stress it until the heart fails. Operating on a seven-year-old boy, Gross tied off the connection to create the necessary separation between the aorta and pulmonary artery and relieve the potentially fatal high blood pressure.

When Taussig read about the groundbreaking operation, her thoughts began to race as an idea took form. Babies with tetralogy of Fallot died because their hearts did not pump enough oxygenated blood throughout their bodies. But if it was possible to tie off a patent ductus arteriosus, why wouldn't it be possible to surgically build an open one to increase the flow of oxygen-rich blood in a blue baby? It seemed so logical to Taussig, she wondered why no one had ever considered the possibility before.

Taussig hurried up to Boston to meet with Gross and proposed that he try this sort of operation. He turned her down flat. "You know," he told her bluntly, "I spent years trying to develop a way to divide the ductus, and now you want me to make one." Taussig tried to laugh off the rejection, but it still stung many years later. "It seemed pretty foolish to him to have me suggest he put a ductus in again," Taussig said. "I think he thought it was one of the craziest things he'd ever heard in a long time."

Dejected but not defeated, Taussig went back to Johns Hopkins and waited for the right opportunity. "When I heard that

Taussig, 1940.

Dr. Alfred Blalock was coming to Baltimore, I thought, 'This is my chance.'" Blalock was known as a skilled surgeon and researcher willing to tackle difficult medical problems; he also had a successful track record. But whether he would be willing to pursue a cure for blue baby syndrome remained to be seen.

CHAPTER FOUR
Answered and Unanswered Questions

EARLY one morning in 1943, the phone in Vivien Thomas's office rang. Thomas was surprised when he answered it and heard the Professor's voice. Blalock never phoned Thomas unless it was an emergency or he had an unusual request. It turned out to be the latter: Dr. Taussig wanted to discuss something related to infant heart defects, and Blalock had arranged for a meeting in the lab.

Thomas had never met Taussig, who headed the pediatric cardiac unit over at the hospital and rarely visited the labs. But he had heard about her from Blalock and the other doctors. Taussig and the female pediatricians on her staff often ruffled the feathers of the male doctors, especially the surgeons. Some of the younger doctors believed that Taussig's clinic was admitting many more young patients than it had in the past. "The perception," reported Laura Malloy, a professor of biology, "was that her clinic was 'robbing' the medical residents in other departments of the opportunity to learn from these cases."

Even when these tensions eased, problems remained. "Dr. Taussig and the other pediatricians would sometimes change the [post-surgery] medication orders [without consulting the surgeon in charge of the case]," Dr. C. Rollins Hanlon observed, "and we would complain to the Professor, and the Professor would speak to Dr. Taussig. It wasn't violent, but there was the usual question of turf when it came to who was running the postoperative care."

"Dr. Taussig could be difficult," Dr. Denton Cooley remembered, "and Dr. Blalock had some friction with her." As Blalock described it to Cooley, "You know, Denton, Dr. Taussig [and her entire staff] come around here and worry me so much."

Taussig "worried" Blalock because she didn't want her ideas (or those of her staff) about the treatment of their patients to be dismissed out of hand. She even "worried" Blalock about how he and his residents treated the parents of her young patients. At the time, most surgeons maintained an authoritarian distance between themselves and their patients. They tended to announce what medical steps would be taken and did not bother to explain the situation to patients or relatives. Taussig insisted that doctors who treated her patients take the extra time and care to explain what was wrong with a child and how they planned to help, be it with medicine or surgery.

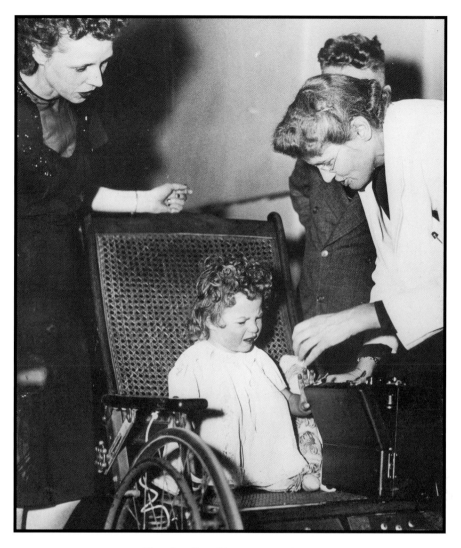

Taussig talks with a young patient.

So on that morning in 1943, Thomas was expecting to meet an intense, possibly brusque Dr. Taussig; instead, he found that she had "a pleasant personality." After introductions, Taussig told Blalock and Thomas about her meeting with Dr. Gross and how she had suggested he reverse his innovative operation to increase the flow of oxygen-rich blood. As Thomas recalled, "She expressed her belief that it should be possible to do something to get more oxygenated blood to the lungs, as a plumber changes pipes around."

This was a remarkable meeting of genius. Taussig was the worldwide expert on congenital heart problems. Blalock, though not a heart specialist, had very good surgical skills and an open mind eager to tackle complex medical problems. He had actually done some research on hypertension (high blood pressure) in the past that involved redirecting the flow of blood to the heart. And finally, there was Vivien Thomas, as determined and brilliant a researcher as anyone at any medical facility.

After Taussig left, Blalock and Thomas continued to discuss the blue baby problem. Because of the war, Blalock's research on shock was still a major national priority; he made this clear to Thomas and instructed him to keep the research on shock as his main focus. But Blalock had promised Taussig that he would look into how to get more oxygen circulating in the bloodstream, so he turned this line of research over to his assistant as well. Thomas would plan and carry out the research, consulting regularly with the Professor and reporting on his results.

Oddly enough, neither man remembered discussing the past hypertension research project as a possible solution to the blue baby problem. Thomas remembered leaving the meeting "sure both of us were aware of what operative procedure was to be tested."

Thomas's first move was to give himself an intensive course in congenital heart problems. He visited the pathology museum to study the many defective hearts that Taussig had collected. "I spent hours and days poring over, examining and studying these preserved specimens," he recalled.

Almost immediately, he perceived just how badly deformed many of the tiny hearts were. He was "amazed that some of these patients had survived as long as they had, or had survived at all." This awareness led to a deeper understanding of Dr. Taussig's intense concern. "If [she] had witnessed the autopsy and examined these numerous hearts, each representing a former patient, one could well appreciate her feeling of utter helplessness."

Taussig had a strong emotional connection to her patients and the pressing sense that time was rapidly running out for them. This bond was what drove her to seek out a solution and "worry" other doctors about treatment and care. Like most surgeons and researchers, Blalock and Thomas chose to remain emotionally separate from the patients, not wanting their feelings to distract them and possibly have a negative effect on their work. Standing in the pathology museum, Thomas understood why Taussig could sometimes be so insistent.

Once Thomas had a clear idea of what the heart of a blue

baby was like, he could move ahead with his research. Before he could think about a cure, he had to figure out how to re-create the condition in a laboratory animal so that he could test various operative procedures on a living creature.

Like many medical researchers at the time, Thomas had done experimental surgery on hundreds and hundreds of dogs in his years with Blalock. With every experiment he conducted using an animal, he entered a world of intense controversy.

Various groups had been actively trying for many years to stop the use of animals in medical research. One of the most powerful organizations was the National Anti-Vivisection Society, founded in 1929. It opposed the use of animals in research experiments for a number of reasons, claiming the practice was immoral (the animals did not volunteer for the experiments and were therefore captives against their will), often caused incredible pain, and almost always ended with the animal either maimed for life or put to death. It also questioned the validity of the experiments because animal bodies did not exactly duplicate human bodies, suggesting that the results were questionable and certainly did not justify the pain and sacrifice of so many animals.

Thomas was well aware of the protests and understood the arguments against the use of animals. He even felt that in some respects the anti-vivisectionists were right. In order to induce shock in one dog, he'd had to crush its leg with a hammer. But

An early-twentieth-century anti-vivisectionist protest in London. There were few crusaders for the cause at first, but their passion helped build the movement into a worldwide force.

he felt strongly that animal testing was a vital part of their research — that, in fact, medical advances could not be made without it.

Back in the 1940s many, if not most, surgeons at Johns Hopkins and at other medical research facilities agreed. Dr. C. Walton (Walt) Lillehei at the University of Minnesota gained worldwide fame in the 1950s by performing the first successful open-heart surgery and helping to develop the first battery-operated pacemaker. When asked about the use of dogs in his research, he was characteristically blunt. "The dog was ideal," he stated, adding, "Without live animals, you got nowhere." Another internationally recognized researcher at the University of Minnesota and chairman of the American Association for Accreditation of Laboratory Animal Care, Dr. Maurice Visscher, minced few words when he said, "I know of no persons of sound mind who doubt that medical research involving surgery of animals has greatly benefited mankind in thousands of ways."

Heart surgery was still in its infancy in 1943. It was such a new branch of medicine that no doctors were listed officially as cardiac surgeons. They were still called thoracic — chest — surgeons, surgeons who could open the chest of a patient to perform various types of procedures, such as draining a lung abscess or removing a tumor. But aside from a few daring individuals, such as Robert Gross, not many surgeons ever attempted any sort of procedure on a living human heart. As the pioneering cardiac surgeon Dr. Harris B. Shumacker points out, very few "clinical efforts in cardiac surgery were undertaken." To be frank, he continues, as late as 1940, "cardiac surgery hardly seemed a viable method of therapy."

In effect, just about everything Thomas and Blalock would

do relating to the human heart would be new and ground-breaking. Even the tools they would eventually use in their procedures would have to be invented and refined as they went along. Back then there were no computers available to create simulated models of the heart or of possible surgical procedures. Adding to the difficulty of devising an operative cure was the fact that no hospital would allow a researcher to use an untested technique on a human subject, even if that human agreed to the procedure. So Thomas had no alternative: experimenting on animals was the only way to find out whether his and Blalock's theories and proposed procedures might actually work on a human.

The debate about the use of animals in medical research projects never faded away as some doctors hoped it would. It has continued through the years right up to the present day. And as computer models and cell testing have become more sophisticated, the demands to end animal testing have intensified. Though fewer animals are involved in medical research today, they are still considered vital for many tests. Even though Thomas was aware of the controversy and sympathized with the protesters to a degree, he could see no other option for creating a new surgical procedure than to test it on animals.

Thomas was embarking on a complicated and uncharted journey. Studying Taussig's preserved hearts had shown him the precise nature of the malformation; he was also able to read about

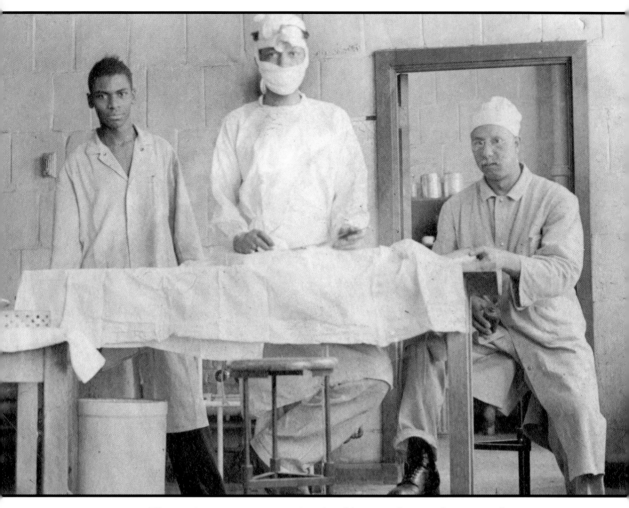

Thomas (*center, wearing surgical mask*) with two assistants, about to perform an experimental procedure on a research dog.

the procedure Gross had performed. These were the only guides available to him. Many more unanswered questions remained to be resolved.

CHAPTER FIVE

The Search

VIVIEN Thomas was a realist. He wanted to find answers to the blue baby problem as quickly as possible without slowing down the shock research. On his own, Thomas came to a decisive conclusion early on. Blalock had made it clear that he didn't want to spend years and years on research that might not lead to a meaningful result; he wanted this part of Thomas's research to be done efficiently and as quickly as possible. Thomas was skilled enough to realize that it could take anywhere from one to two years to reproduce all four tetralogy of Fallot problems in an animal. Instead, Thomas suggested they concentrate solely on reducing the flow of oxygenated blood throughout the animal's body. He had to make a healthy animal unhealthy.

Blalock was not happy about this. It meant that they would not be working for a total cure to the problem, only a partial fix. But Thomas was certain that in time he could replicate the most serious defect that Taussig had identified, that of limiting the flow of oxygen to the dog's body. With this as his focus, Thomas plunged forward with his experiments.

Simply restricting the flow of oxygen-rich blood wouldn't be enough. Thomas had to lower the amount of blood oxygen to a precise level, as close as possible to the low level of oxygen in blue babies. He had data on what this level was from Taussig's research, and he analyzed the blood of a number of blue babies to verify past results. In addition to re-creating the exact level of oxygen depletion, the experimental animals would have to survive with this lower oxygen level for many days before any sort of corrective procedure could be attempted. Thomas and Blalock wanted the animals to recover from the initial surgery and duplicate as nearly as possible what a blue baby experienced.

Thomas's first attempts to control the blood oxygen level were very simple, even crude. He took a piece of sterile linen cord and tied off the artery leading from the lung to the heart. He performed this procedure on a number of animals, tying the cord a little tighter on each one to restrict the flow of oxygenated blood to just the right level. These attempts all failed because the cord very quickly began to cut into the delicate artery.

Over the following weeks and months, Thomas experimented with a series of other materials — rubber tubing, surgical tape, a silver clamp, even a strip of ox tissue — to see if they would restrict oxygen without damaging the artery. Nothing worked.

After this, with Blalock's advice, Thomas tried other increasingly complex ways to reduce oxygen levels. He rerouted unoxygenated blood from the right side of a dog's heart to the left side, which meant the blood never went to the lungs. He did this by connecting the pulmonary artery and vein on the right side

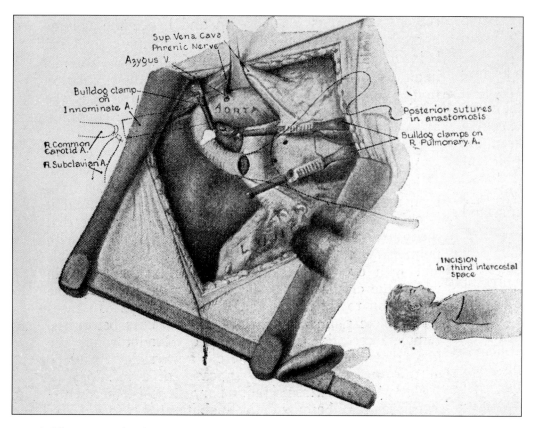

As Thomas was developing the blue baby procedure by operating on dogs, he was envisioning what it would be like to perform it on a human patient and trying to anticipate potential problems. This detailed medical drawing shows the small opening and very crowded space inside the chest of a child, where Blalock would have to do delicate cutting and suturing.

of the heart. The procedure produced lower oxygenation, but the animals died when fluid backed up in their lungs.

Next, he removed sections of the lung and rerouted the pulmonary artery and vein. None of these attempts succeeded. Blalock and Thomas had to devise other surgical ways to produce lower oxygen levels.

While this line of research went on, Thomas was also working on other practical aspects of the operation. A baby's arteries and veins are so tiny — often no bigger than a thin wire — that Thomas had to practice making precise, even sutures. Because the blood vessels of a medium-sized dog's heart are so tiny, they proved to be very good for this sort of training.

Everyone who ever worked with Thomas praised his skills as a surgeon. Thomas was so demanding of himself, so insistent that nothing short of perfection was acceptable, that his ability as a surgeon went beyond good or even very good. His skills were nothing short of miraculous. Once Thomas was finishing up an experimental procedure when Blalock came in. Blalock looked at the artery that had been reattached and could see only one tiny piece of thread as evidence that anything had happened. Thomas had sewn the artery on the inside so that absolutely nothing could be seen on the outside besides where the silk had been tied off. Amazed, Blalock shook his head and mumbled that Thomas's work was so close to perfect that it might have been "something the Lord had made."

Besides perfecting his skills, Thomas also had to design new or improved surgical equipment. Few commercial manufacturers of surgical tools existed at the time. The giant pharmaceutical company Johnson & Johnson had been in business since 1886, but a surgical products unit was not set up until 1941, and it offered only a limited line of items. This forced Thomas to study all the surgical tools that would be needed for the operation and come up with ways to adapt and improve them. When the clamps Thomas was using to close off an artery began to slip, Dr. Longmire (who had assisted at the first surgery) and Thomas created one that screwed closed to provide just the right amount of pressure. Because Blalock was always considered the lead researcher on the blue baby project, the clamp came to be known as the Blalock clamp. Johnson & Johnson sold suturing needles with silk already through the eye. But the needles were too long for the intricate sewing Thomas was doing. So Thomas had to cut them down to the size he needed and sharpen the points himself.

Adding to the pressure on Thomas was the knowledge that more and more severely ill children were being admitted to the hospital. Taussig could worry about them and try her best to help them; Blalock could tell her that progress was being made on

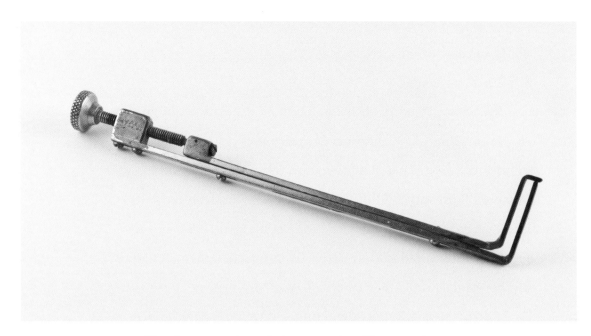

After clamps came loose during a procedure, Thomas and Longmire created what was later called the Blalock clamp.

devising a surgical procedure, even if slowly. But Thomas knew that the responsibility of developing a workable procedure was his.

Almost a year into the blue baby research, Thomas had carried out over one hundred experiments and was logging fourteen- to fifteen-hour days, often seven days a week — one failed attempt to create a low oxygen level after another. Yet each failure brought him a step closer to the results he was searching for. Along the way, Thomas began experimenting with a surgical solution to increase oxygen level in the blood.

Here is where the collective knowledge and skill of Blalock and Thomas made a decisive difference. In 1938, while they were still at Vanderbilt, they had tried to create high blood pressure in an animal by attaching an artery leaving the heart to an artery leading to the lungs. They wanted to see if adding so much more oxygen to the blood would create this condition. The procedure did elevate oxygen levels in the blood but didn't increase blood pressure. This failure didn't mean the experiment was useless, however. As Professor Robert B. Pond, an authority on scientific creativity, has observed, "It is completely possible to invent something and never know what the need is, never know what problem you had solved."

Thomas began reworking and refining the failed high blood pressure procedure, hoping to send more oxygenated blood to the heart. This phase of the research went relatively quickly because Thomas had performed the operation many times at Vanderbilt. But it still required numerous repetitions over several months, mainly because Blalock insisted that all results (such as measuring oxygen levels before and after the procedure) be checked multiple times for accuracy.

Besides, there were still many unanswered questions. Some of the animal subjects had suffered temporary paralysis following the operation. Would the same happen to a human subject? Would a blue baby tolerate anesthesia? Would clamping shut the artery carrying oxygenated blood cause brain damage? What other problems might arise? Despite these lingering concerns, toward the end of summer 1944, Thomas was able to say with satisfaction, "As Dr. Taussig had hoped, we, like plumbers, had 'changed the pipes' around to get more blood to the lungs. We had found what pipes to put where."

Now it was time for Vivien Thomas to teach Alfred Blalock how to rearrange the pipes.

CHAPTER SIX

"All the World Is Against It"

ALFRED Blalock was a stickler when it came to being thoroughly prepared for every aspect of his work. Now that Thomas had worked out the blue baby procedure (with, as Thomas himself admitted, the necessary assistance of Blalock's "brain power in this as in all the other projects"), Blalock wanted the chance to practice it on a number of animals before actually performing surgery on a human. He considered this the only way to avoid a fatal mistake.

The world-famous heart surgeon Denton A. Cooley worked closely with the Professor during that period and understood why he felt a need to practice a procedure so many times. "He was insecure as a technical surgeon," Cooley observed years later, "and he wasn't really adept and sure of himself all the time." Dr. J. Alex Haller Jr. joined Johns Hopkins in the late 1940s and worked side by side with Blalock in the operating room for many years.

Dr. J. Alex Haller worked very closely with Blalock for many years.

He concurred with Cooley's appraisal. Blalock "was very meticulous in the operating room, a good technician, but not a brilliant technician."

There was more occupying Blalock's mind than most people suspected at the time. Blalock had grown up in a well-to-do family, gone to private schools, and done really well despite not being an avid scholar. Even when in college studying to be a doctor, according to his best friend and roommate, Tinsley Harrison,

Blalock was much more interested in competitive sports and going to parties with pretty girls than in preparing for exams. But Blalock graduated, and he and Harrison went on to Johns Hopkins to complete their medical education.

What changed Blalock from a playboy into a dedicated scientist? He never explained this in his writings, but we can piece together a plausible explanation. When he finished his studies, he applied to Johns Hopkins for a surgical residency, a position that would let him work side by side with the best surgeons in the country. He was promptly rejected, in large part because of his reputation for partying.

He was given a residency at Vanderbilt and after a year was also put in charge of the research laboratory. He was making real progress with his research on shock when he developed tuberculosis and was forced to rest and get treatment for months at a time. Other researchers kept his experiments moving at Vanderbilt, but Blalock felt he was a failure — both for not getting a residency at Johns Hopkins and because his illness limited his ability to work — and he feared he was being left behind as a researcher.

When his TB went into remission, Blalock returned to work, but he knew that the disease could come roaring back in a month or a year and incapacitate or even kill him. He became determined to make his mark as a serious researcher as quickly as possible. When he was made head of surgery and research at Johns

Hopkins, he felt that his heightened focus on advancing medicine had been justified. Still, his desire to push research projects forward — before his own time ran out — was always tempered by his fear that a miscalculation or lack of preparation might result in failure and dismissal.

Thomas began preparing a dog for a test operation in which he, Thomas, would be the lead surgeon and Blalock would assist. This meant that Thomas would actually perform the operation while Blalock stood next to him to observe what happened, help Thomas when needed, and ask any questions he might have. After this, Blalock would be the lead surgeon on at least two additional research operations with Thomas assisting and advising.

The procedure in which Blalock assisted went exactly as they had hoped. Then Eileen Saxon arrived at Johns Hopkins on Monday, November 27, and Blalock's careful preparation plan was derailed.

Eileen had an extremely advanced case of blue baby syndrome. At eighteen months, she was twelve pounds underweight and very tiny, with her lips, fingernails, and skin a dark, sickly blue. Worse, she was gasping for air and seemed to be on the verge of heart failure.

All Dr. Taussig could do to help the child was put her in an oxygen tent and hope her condition stabilized and improved. But it was clear that Eileen was still in distress, and Taussig worried that the girl's oxygen-deprived heart would give out in a day or two, if not sooner. Blalock had informed Taussig that Thomas had succeeded in developing a workable procedure to help her blue babies, and now she contacted Blalock and told him his first human patient had arrived.

Blalock was unwilling to operate. He wasn't prepared, he

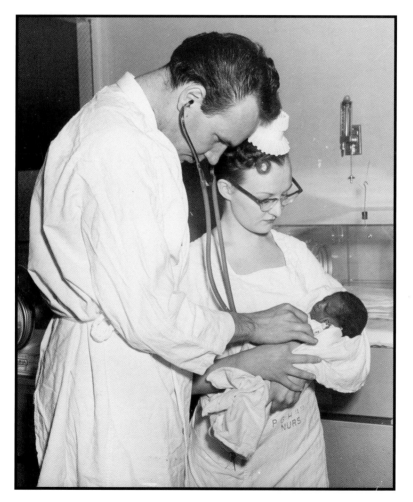

Denton A. Cooley checks the condition of a patient.

insisted. He needed time — possibly several weeks — to master the innovative procedure. But Taussig wasn't about to take no for an answer, not when there was the slightest chance of saving her patient. So, reluctantly, Blalock agreed to schedule the surgery.

Once Blalock agreed to the operation, he and everyone else involved knew that the clock was ticking.

He asked Thomas to set up the operating room with all of the necessary implements and equipment and began assembling his surgical team. Blalock requested that Drs. Longmire and Cooley participate, and also a scrub nurse, Charlotte Mitchell. She would be beside Blalock during the operation to hand him instruments and wipe away blood. Taussig, too, would be in the operating room to watch over her patient. Finally, Blalock asked the head of Johns Hopkins anesthesiology, Dr. Austin Lamont, to administer the anesthesia that would keep Eileen from feeling pain during the procedure.

When Dr. Lamont examined Eileen Saxon, he balked at the idea of operating on her. He was convinced that the tiny patient wouldn't survive being anesthetized and, if she somehow miraculously did, wouldn't live through the actual operation.

Lamont may have been concerned that killing such a young patient might damage his professional reputation. At best this was a chancy operation, and many of his colleagues might have questioned the wisdom of attempting it in the first place. But

Lamont was known as an especially caring doctor, and he was probably eager to spare Eileen any unnecessary pain. Like most other doctors, Lamont wouldn't consider necessary an experimental operation that had little chance of succeeding, under any circumstances. As Lamont would say later, "When suffering becomes unbearable, nature often lifts the burden." That is, sometimes a patient should be allowed to die, and in his opinion Eileen was such a patient.

This was a reasonable position back in 1944. Nowadays, it is common practice not just to operate on human hearts, but to remove a diseased and damaged heart and replace it with either a mechanical device or a donated human heart. Back then, however, the heart was considered untouchable.

This idea had a very long history. For centuries, the common belief was that to merely touch a beating human heart could cause it to stop working. To cut into one was generally viewed as reckless and possibly even criminal. Even after a fellow surgeon successfully sewed up a stab wound to the heart in 1896, Dr. Stephen Paget was not convinced that operating on a beating heart was possible. "Surgery of the heart," Paget wrote, "has probably reached the limit set by nature to all such surgery. No new method and no new discovery can overcome the natural difficulties that attend a wound of the heart." In the early 1940s one historian summed up the prevailing attitude: "The heart was

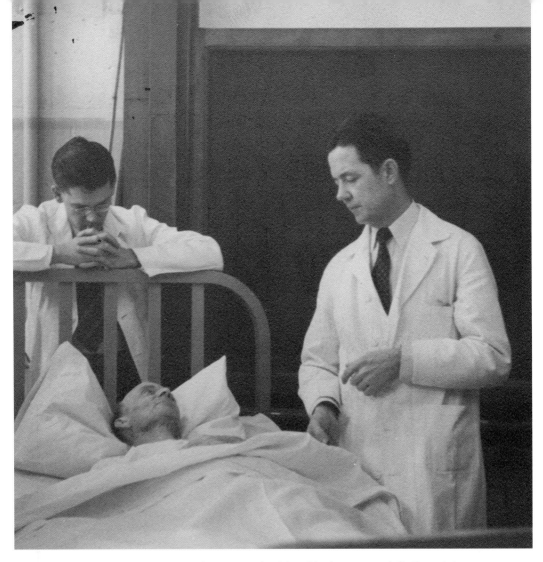

Blalock was responsible for running the Johns Hopkins research facility, a job that involved a great deal of administrative work, such as drawing up budgets and hiring staff. His passions, however, were research, caring for patients, and teaching medical students.

considered too critical, too vital, too complex and delicate to permit surgery or other invasive techniques."

Blalock respected Lamont's opinion and did not press him to be a part of his surgical team. Instead, he turned to Merel

Harmel, a highly skilled anesthesiologist just a year out of medical school. The young doctor thought the operation was risky, but he also felt that any intelligent attempt to save a patient's life was acceptable. Once Harmel was on board, the operation was rescheduled for the next day.

As head of surgery, Blalock had the authority to okay the operation without seeking approval from anyone else. He did, however, advise the director of Johns Hopkins Hospital that he planned to go forward with the surgery and that Taussig supported his decision.

Thomas and the hospital operating room supervisor, Elizabeth Sherwood, continued to ready room 706 and assemble the necessary instruments. Additional lighting had to be brought in, as well as tanks of oxygen, sheets for the operating table, gauze, and everything else that might be needed. Thomas had cut six 1⅛-inch-long needles down to ½ inch. Then he threaded the eye of each with silk thread and, using a spring-type clothespin to hold the needle, he sharpened each by hand on an emery board. Very little about the operating room or instruments would be considered innovative or even safe today.

Taussig met with Blalock early that evening to discuss Eileen's condition. It hadn't improved, she told him, and the baby seemed to be in somewhat greater distress than earlier in the day. Taussig urged the Professor to go home and get some rest. She

Dr. William Longmire assisted Blalock during the first blue baby operation even though he feared that the tiny patient might not tolerate anesthesia.

stayed at the hospital all night to monitor Eileen and comfort her parents.

Blalock felt he wasn't as prepared for this operation as he would have liked. He also knew that every phase of the procedure—from the diagnosis, to the operating conditions, to the postoperative care—was primitive at best. Others agreed with him in hindsight. Dr. William Stoney, a medical historian, noted, "This was an operation that was done before most of the technology to make it easier and safer was available." Dr. Cooley was even more direct: "Many of us thought this operation was going to be a big disaster."

Blalock knew that once he had agreed to perform the operation he had no choice but to move forward. Eileen was slowly dying, and the procedure was her only chance at survival. While his reasoning was accurate, it didn't make him less anxious. He never recorded his thoughts, but another cardiac surgical researcher, Dr. Charles Bailey, may have captured something of Blalock's emotional state: "You know that almost all the world is against it; you know that you have a great personal stake and might even lose your medical license if you persist. In fact, the thought crosses your mind that maybe you really *are* crazy. And yet you feel that it has to be done and it must be right."

CHAPTER SEVEN

"Vivien, You'd Better Come Down Here"

THE next day, Wednesday, November 29, Blalock was so anxious that he felt he couldn't drive himself to the hospital and asked his wife to take him. He entered the great domed building, crossed the rotunda, and (following Johns Hopkins tradition) rubbed the toe of the statue of Christ for good luck. Then he went to see how Eileen was doing.

Thomas had arrived earlier to make sure the operating room and surgical supplies were ready. Then he retreated to the laboratory. When a colleague asked if he would observe the operation from the viewing area, Thomas replied that Blalock "had said nothing about my being there" and added jokingly that he "might make Dr. Blalock nervous or even worse, he might make me nervous."

Just moments before Eileen was to be wheeled into the operating room, Blalock entered room 706 and glanced around. Then he looked up into the viewing area and spotted one of his assistants, Clara Belle Puryear. "Miss Puryear," Blalock said, "I guess you better go call Vivien."

Thomas appeared in the gallery a few minutes later, but that wasn't what Blalock wanted. "Vivien, you'd better come down here," he said in his soft southern drawl. Blalock was so insecure about the operation that he wanted Thomas near him to observe and advise him if necessary.

As the rest of the surgical team assembled, Thomas

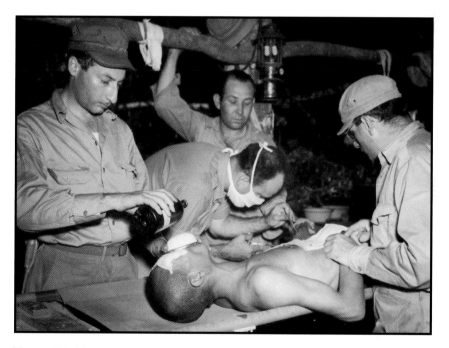

Here, a World War II medic administers anesthetic to a wounded soldier. The "open anesthesia" method would be used during the first blue baby operation. The anesthetic would be dripped through a fine mesh so that the patient inhaled its fumes. This meant that the anesthesiologist had to guess when enough had been administered. Not enough would mean the patient might wake during surgery; too much could kill the patient.

positioned himself just behind Blalock on a small wooden step stool, which allowed him to see over Blalock's shoulder. It is safe to say that no other surgeon in the United States, let alone a southern surgeon, had ever had an African American research assistant monitoring his every move so publicly.

When Eileen was wheeled in, Thomas recalled, "The patient [was so small] it was difficult to ascertain whether [she] was beneath the sterile drapes." Dr. Harmel administered the anesthesia. When this was complete and everyone was certain Eileen would feel no pain, Blalock went to work.

Using a scalpel, Blalock made a curving four-inch incision in the left side of Eileen's chest, cutting first through the skin, then a thin layer of fat. He paused to study the small amount of blood that oozed from the cut. It was dark and syrupy thick, a sign that there was little oxygen in it. Next, he used a metal device called a rib spreader to separate the patient's ribs, and held them apart with a clamp. Finally, he cut through a tough membrane, called the pleura, that lines the chest cavity. This was done slowly and painstakingly. After each step Blalock paused to be sure Eileen was still breathing normally.

Inside the chest cavity Blalock encountered his first problem: light. Or rather, a lack of it. A four-inch opening doesn't allow much light to enter the chest cavity, and the tight space

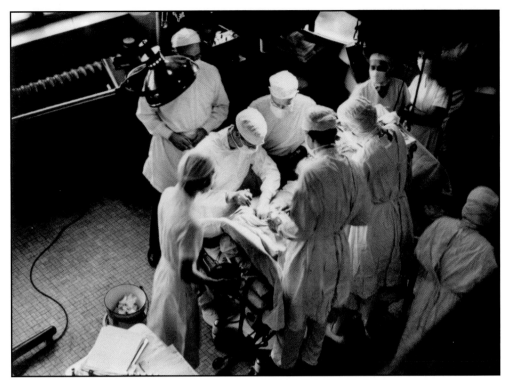
An overhead view of a blue baby operation. Thomas is standing just behind
Blalock, partially hidden by the lamp.

and shadows made every cut of the scalpel potentially dangerous.
When surgery took place on gloomy days, Blalock often dragged a
common floor lamp with an ordinary incandescent bulb into the
operating room to add a bit more light. The lamp that Thomas
had brought in the day before was moved closer and focused on
the incision, and Blalock was able to proceed.

When he reached Eileen's heart, he and Thomas saw their
second problem. Eileen's arteries were, in Thomas's words, "less
than half the size of vessels of the experimental animals that had

been used to develop the procedure." Thomas had done his experimental surgeries on dogs that were easily twice Eileen's size, so their arteries and veins were proportionally bigger.

Because the arteries of very young children are so small, Blalock would refuse to operate on patients as young as Eileen in the future. But it was too late now to back out. Eileen's physical strength was already compromised by the opening of her chest. To stop the operation would not lessen her weakness in any way and certainly wouldn't help her oxygenate her blood.

While Blalock hesitated, Thomas leaned in for a closer look. Dr. Cooley remembered, "Dr. Blalock would ask Vivien questions over his shoulder. He would say, 'Vivien, should I do it this way or that way?' Vivien would know the answers as he was used to having those kinds of questions put to him."

Moving very cautiously, Blalock began the most serious work of the operation. He clamped a branch of the aorta shut. After pausing to see if the patient was tolerating this, he cut the clamped section free of the surrounding tissue and was able to move it close to the pulmonary artery.

Next Blalock cut into the pulmonary artery and began the painstaking process of suturing the end of the aortic branch to it. "I watched closely as each suture was placed," Thomas recalled. In order to hold the aorta and pulmonary artery securely together, the sutures had to be no more than one millimeter (approximately the thickness of a dime) apart. "If he began a suture in the wrong direction (which he did on several occasions), I would say, 'the other direction.'"

Reading about the blue baby operation takes only a few minutes. Blalock's postoperative account is a mere one and a half pages. But the actual operation took more than an hour and a half to complete. Blalock's delicate work of cutting and suturing "was all done with some difficulty but with great skill," Dr. Longmire noted. "Dr. Blalock's surgical skill has been questioned, but if you could have seen him complete [this] difficult operation you would recognize that the skill was there."

The joining of the two arteries was complete and seemed to be a success, but Blalock did not immediately close up Eileen's chest. He used two fingers to feel the pulmonary artery and was "disturbed because I could not feel a thrill," meaning he couldn't feel the movement of blood through the artery.

Blalock, Thomas, Taussig, and the rest of the surgical team, as well as the gallery watchers, all paused, hushed and quite literally holding their breath. It was entirely possible to perform a perfect operation and yet have the patient die.

Then the anesthesiologist, Merel Harmel, looked at Eileen's face and said in an excited whisper, "The color is improving." A few seconds later he added even more urgently, "Take a look. Take a look."

OPERATION: Nov. 29, 1944
          Dr. Alfred Blalock
          Ether - Oxygen - Dr. Harmel

ANASTOMOSIS OF LEFT PULMONARY ARTERY TO LEFT SUBCLAVIAN ARTERY

          This patient was an undernourished child who had cyanosis on fre-
quent occasions. The diagnosis was pulmonary stenosis.

          Under ether and oxygen, administered by the open method, an incision
was made in the left chest extending from the edge of the sternum to the ax-
illary line in the third interspace. The second and third costal cartilages
were divided. The pleural cavity was entered. The left lung looked normal.
No thrill was felt in palpating the heart and pulmonary artery. The left pulmonary artery was identified and was dissected free of the neighboring tissues.
The left pulmonary artery seemed to be of normal size. The superior pulmonary
vein, on the other hand, seemed considerably smaller than normal to me. I had
hoped that the artery to the left upper lobe might be sufficiently long to
allow an anastomosis, but this did not appear to be the case. The left subclavian artery was then identified and was dissected free of the neighboring
tissues. The vertebral artery and the branches of the thyrocervical axis were
doubly ligated and divided. The subclavian was so short that there would not
have been sufficient length for our purposes, had this not been done. The subclavian artery was then ligated distal to the thyrocervical trunk. A bulldog
clip was placed on the subclavian artery at a point just distal to its origin
from the aorta. The subclavian artery was then divided just proximal to the
ligature. Two bulldog clips were then placed on the left pulmonary artery, the
first clip being placed at the origin of the left pulmonary artery, and the
second clip being placed just proximal to the point where the artery entered
the lung. There was ample space between these two clips for our purpose. A
small transverse incision was then made in the wall of the pulmonary artery.
By the use of china beaded silk on fine needles, an anastomosis was then performed between the end of the left subclavian artery and the side of the left
pulmonary artery. A posterior row of sutures was placed first. There was
practically no bleeding following the removal of the bulldog clips.

          The anastomosis seemed to be a satisfactory one, and the main point
of worry comes from the small size of the left subclavian artery. I was disturbed because I could not feel a thrill in the pulmonary artery after the
clips were removed. I do not believe that this was due to any clot in the
subclavian artery, because it seemed to pulsate vigorously. It is possible
that it was due to a low pressure in the systemic circulation. I do not actually
know what the systemic pressure was. Another possibility was that it might
have been due to spasm of the subclavian artery. My only regret was that the
subclavian artery was not bigger. It is possible that the increased red
cell count in this patient may have predisposed to thrombosis.

                                                            (over)

Blalock's hand-typed notes about the first blue baby operation.

Dr. William Stoney recounted that Blalock, Taussig, and Longmire all "leaned over . . . and looked at the child's face." Instead of ashen skin and sickly blue lips, they now "saw the cherry-

Sulfanilamide was placed in the left pleural cavity.
This was followed by closure of the incision in the chest wall.
The third and fourth ribs were approximated by two encircling
sutures of braided silk. The soft tissues of the wall were closed
in layers with silk sutures.

The patient stood the procedure better than I had
anticipated. It is interesting that the cyanosis did not appear
to increase very greatly from the temporary occlusion of the left
pulmonary artery. It is also of interest that the circulation
in the nail beds of the left hand appeared to be fairly good at
the completion of the operation.

I did not attempt to visualize the left common carotid
artery. It is possible that this would have been bigger than the
left subclavian. This child was very small and I am confident
that the subclavian artery would be more easily dealt with in a
larger child.

(Dr. Blalock)
ms

red color of her lips. It was astounding how quickly the child's
color improved. It was really quite dramatic."

Longmire would add that the entire team were beside

themselves with joy that the operation — one that many thought would fail — had indeed worked. Yet Blalock and his team still had plenty to do. They dosed the newly connected arteries and surrounding area with sulfanilamide, a common antibacterial used to fight off infection, then began the painstaking work of sewing their tiny patient back together. Eventually, the incision was closed and Blalock and his colleagues could lean back and take a deep, relaxing breath. The operation was not just complete; it was a success.

CHAPTER EIGHT

Then What Happened?

ONCE the operation was over, Eileen Saxon was whisked to her crib in a fourth-floor hospital room, where she would be constantly monitored by a doctor and a team of nurses. Every so often, Blalock or Taussig came by to check on their young patient.

There wouldn't have been much any of the doctors could do if something did go wrong. At the time, aside from the sulfanilamide splashed on the wound after the procedure, and orally administered penicillin, very few drugs existed to treat infections. There were no defibrillators to shock a failed heart back into action, and no drugs to slow a rapidly beating heart. In 1957 the British surgeon Dr. Geoffrey Wooler lamented that so many patients were dying in the days following heart operations "because of the lack of modern postoperative care. [Doctors] did not have an intensive care unit, no ventilator, and no [blood circulation] monitoring." And conditions were far more primitive back in the 1940s.

There were some rough moments for Eileen in the days after surgery. She would suddenly begin gasping for air, and the attending doctor had to give her oxygen until her breathing returned to normal. "Eileen's recovery was not as smooth or as rapid as we had hoped," Thomas noted, "but after two weeks of intensive care, her condition improved. Improvement continued, and after almost two months she was released. . . . Her complexion, no longer ashen blue, was an almost normal pink."

With Thomas standing right behind him and Taussig watching carefully, Blalock performed two additional blue baby operations in early February 1945. Both the twelve-year-old girl and the six-year-old boy showed immediate and dramatic improvement.

After this, Blalock and Taussig wrote a detailed, scholarly article about the operations that appeared in a major medical journal. The brief article had an amazing impact on Blalock, Taussig, Johns Hopkins, and the world of medicine. Within days of its May 1945 publication, surgeons from all over the United States were calling, asking to observe the new procedure. A few weeks later, as news spread, doctors from around the world began contacting Johns Hopkins.

Magazine and newspaper reporters wrote about the remark-

A newspaper article about the blue baby operation and two children who were saved by it.

able operation in which a child who was literally blue one moment suddenly began to take on a pink, healthy glow — and the information was seized by the public. Soon parents with blue babies began appearing at the doors of Johns Hopkins. "Some of the parents did not bother to [consult] their doctors," Thomas said. "They came by automobile, train, and plane. Many had not communicated with the hospital, had no appointment in the clinic, and had no hotel reservations; the cardiac clinic was overrun with patients." But every child brought to the hospital was taken in and given a bed.

Both Blalock and Taussig were astonished by the dramatic reaction. They had hoped the procedure would be successful and be duplicated again and again—and that it would save lives. But the national and international response was overwhelming. Thomas knew why. "To these parents, this operation was their great hope; this was what they had been praying for."

At first, the attention embarrassed Blalock. He had a strong enough ego, but he never clamored for personal attention. Besides, at the time it was considered unseemly for a surgeon, even the head of a surgical department, to appear in too many newspaper or magazine articles. But the demand for more and more information about the operation continued. Soon Blalock was traveling to Europe to demonstrate the procedure. On a 1945 visit to Great Britain, Blalock and Taussig gave a series of speeches to various medical groups. Dr. Russell Brock was astonished when he tried to attend one lecture and found it "literally impossible to enter the building by the time the lecture was about to start" because of the overflowing crowd.

Dr. Brock did manage to get into the lecture Blalock and Taussig gave to the British Medical Association a few days later. The Great Hall was packed, he wrote in a letter afterward, and Dr. Taussig delivered a precise description of congenital heart abnormalities and of the work she had done with Dr. Blalock. Blalock

Blalock with his surgical house staff, 1945.

spoke next, delivering "a forceful and impressive presentation" about the technical aspects of the operation and the results.

Blalock delivered his remarks in a subdued voice, and the audience listened in absolute silence to his every word. Dr. Brock recalled that the hall was quite dark because Blalock presented a series of slides with his talk. When Blalock finished, "A long searchlight beam traversed the whole length of the hall and unerringly picked out on the platform a [nurse] sitting on a chair holding a small cherub-like girl of 2½ years with a halo of blonde

Blalock and Taussig, 1946.

curly hair and looking pink and well; she had been operated on by Blalock a week earlier."

The audience sat in silence looking at the child for a moment or two. Another physician who was there, Dr. Alex Haller, remembered, "There was a sort of awe, then a quiet, and then there was this emotional upheaval and outstanding applause. A lot of people realized that this was a very significant breakthrough."

The somewhat shy and reclusive Blalock was already internationally famous for his life-saving work on the causes and treatment of shock. The blue baby operation had made him as well known as any star of stage or screen, the most famous cardiac surgeon of his generation.

The impact of the blue baby operation on Johns Hopkins was "more than a flood of patients with congenital heart disease," Dr. William Stoney observed. "It also brought a succession of talented and creative young surgical residents, most of whom went on to distinguished careers in other medical schools. The blue baby operation and all that came with it reestablished the Hopkins program as the premier surgical training program of the era."

Other research hospitals in the United States and around the world noticed this sudden intense interest in cardiac problems. Those that already had budding heart research programs began to increase their budgets. Other hospitals opened research programs of their own, many headed by doctors who had worked with Blalock and Thomas at Johns Hopkins. These facilities not only conducted research in new surgical procedures, but in time they also pioneered such innovative medical devices as artificial hearts, defibrillators, and the heart-lung machine.

By the time they had performed the third blue baby operation, Blalock and Thomas realized they wouldn't be able to repeat the procedure often if Thomas had to make all the special surgical equipment needed every time. Thomas thought the problem over and, as always, devised an efficient and simple plan. He went

After the operation, Blalock became a superstar of heart surgery, and newspapers and magazines asked for photographs. Here he poses with a photograph of one of his patients.

to various local manufacturers and paid them to produce the required needles, silk thread, clamps, and other items.

The decision was a wise one. Once word about the operation went public and patients began arriving in droves, Blalock and the surgeons under him began doing blue baby operations regularly. By 1950, one thousand such operations had been performed at Johns Hopkins alone.

Over the following years, medical suppliers noticed the sea change in cardiac surgery and research and began producing a wide variety of surgical devices. From a handful of manufacturers offering a limited number of items in 1945, the industry grew steadily as more and more innovative surgical procedures were introduced. Today, more than 1,300 companies produce surgical devices in the United States alone, with combined annual sales of over $42 billion.

Helen Taussig had her fair share of fame as well. As they had in England, she and Blalock often paired up to give lectures on congenital heart abnormalities and the blue baby operation. She also lectured widely on other pediatric heart problems and went on to write two definitive books on congenital heart defects that are still in use today, as well as 129 scientific articles. She would head the pediatric cardiology

Johnson & Johnson was an important manufacturer in 1947, when this advertisement for baby powder and baby oil appeared. Once medical research teams were established in universities and hospitals around the country during the 1950s, the company would grow into an international giant.

When Taussig retired in 1963, the doctors who had trained with her commissioned the young artist Jamie Wyeth to paint her portrait. The result startled and disappointed everyone because she looked severe, almost witchlike, in the painting. Taussig appreciated the gesture but never hung up the picture.

unit at Johns Hopkins for more than thirty years and was one of the first doctors in the United States to recognize and lobby against the use of the drug thalidomide by pregnant women because it could cause severe birth defects.

For her many accomplishments, Taussig received an astonishing number of awards and honors for a woman in a male-dominated occupation—twenty honorary degrees from medical schools, more than thirty major medical awards, and the Medal of Freedom, the highest honor that can be given to an American citizen. In presenting this award in 1964, President Lyndon B.

Johnson said of Taussig, "Physician, physiologist and embryologist, her fundamental concepts have made possible the modern surgery of the heart."

Oddly enough, in the aftermath, a number of doctors and medical historians minimized her contribution to the research and the operation. Some suggested that Taussig merely asked Blalock if there might be a surgical way to provide more oxygen; others implied that she added nothing to the research. This wasn't true, of course, and Alfred Blalock was the first to praise her expertise and contributions. It was Taussig, Blalock noted in

Taussig (*back row, center*) with members of her staff as President Lyndon B. Johnson awarded her the Medal of Freedom, the highest honor that can be bestowed upon an American civilian, in 1964.

their report, who figured out that oxygen depletion needed to be reversed, an understanding that "led to the clinical work recorded in this paper." Blalock, it seemed, was willing to share the credit, even if some other colleagues were not as generous.

Meanwhile, Vivien Thomas went back to the laboratory. There was work to be done on shock and other projects that Blalock had put in motion, and the blue baby operation needed refinement. After the first procedure, Blalock and Thomas conferred on how to avoid the problems they had encountered and how to improve the results. They wanted to take a good operation and make it better. The next two operations were both a little different from the first, which meant Thomas had to work out the details in the lab beforehand.

What did Thomas think about the frantic media attention and worldwide fame Blalock, Taussig, and Johns Hopkins received during the months and years after the blue baby operation? No one will ever know. Thomas left behind no written record about this and never said anything to colleagues or friends about his feelings. He was a reserved and quiet man, not used to drawing attention to himself or to complaining.

But it would be entirely understandable if he felt some level of resentment. After all, he had spent thousands of hours working on the procedure, almost all of the time by himself. Blalock and Taussig clearly made vital contributions to the research, but

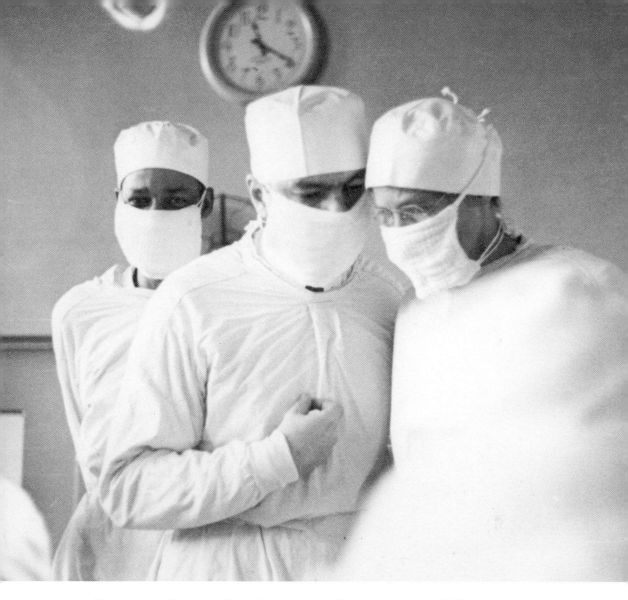

Taussig (*right*) discussing a blue baby operation with a visiting surgeon, 1947.
Thomas (*background, left*) is waiting to advise his colleagues.

Thomas was as much the creator of the blue baby operation as they were. And yet he wasn't mentioned in the Blalock-Taussig journal article or in any of their lectures or magazine articles on the operation.

Portrait of Anna by DeNyse W. Turner, 1951. Anna was the first animal subject to survive the experimental blue baby procedure.

Over the following years Thomas watched quietly as many young surgeons—whom he had helped to train—went on to highly successful careers and fame at other research facilities. Even one of the research dogs, Anna, received more immediate attention than did Thomas. The first animal subject to survive the operation, Anna had an honored place in the lab, where she wandered around freely for nearly fifteen years. She was frequently photographed for magazine articles along with children who had had the operation, and a movie was made about her in 1950. In 1951, her portrait was painted and presented to Johns Hopkins Hospital, where it still hangs today.

Was Thomas being overlooked because he was African American? At the time, research assistants (no matter the color of their skin) were often overlooked when it came to credit for a breakthrough discovery. Because they weren't doctors, they were viewed as hired workers who simply followed the instructions of the physician running the laboratory or directing a particular line of research. The assistant might offer a suggestion or an opinion, but, it was assumed, very few took a creative part in formulating or carrying out research.

There were exceptions, of course. There always are. And Vivien Thomas was a prime example. When Thomas began working for Blalock, he was instructed by the Professor and other surgeons on how to perform various complicated medical procedures and keep accurate records of the results. He was clearly under the careful guidance of others during his first few years. Over time, however, Thomas began doing precisely what Blalock had requested during Thomas's initial job interview: he got "to the point that he [could] do things on his own."

In all likelihood, when Blalock said this he was hoping that he could give Thomas an assignment and that Thomas would carry it out, not needing to continually bother him with questions. But Thomas had been raised by two parents who encouraged problem solving, whether that involved sewing a particularly complicated clothes pattern or finding a way to repair a house. Thomas did exactly the same thing in the laboratory. Shown how to do a surgical procedure, he

Thomas pauses during a busy day.

would master it and then find ways to make it simpler or better. As Dr. Henry Bahnson, a colleague of Blalock's, recalled, "Dr. Blalock taught Vivien a lot, but Vivien also discovered a lot of new techniques himself and taught them to Dr. Blalock."

Even so, many doctors and historians believe Thomas was a victim of discrimination. When discussing the way people behaved toward Thomas after the operation, Dr. Levi Watkins Jr. didn't mince words: "Vivien was not a co-equal by any stretch of the imagination."

Watkins didn't say or suggest that Blalock was a racist. He did say, "I think the gentlemen both were products of their time." Blalock may have hesitated to highlight Thomas's many achievements because he feared a backlash from racially biased colleagues at the school, which would have hindered his research, or from his relatives and neighbors, which might have made him and his family feel uncomfortable and isolated. He also may have worried that letting the world know about Thomas and his miraculous skills would result in job offers from competing research laboratories.

For his part, Thomas may have hesitated to assert himself, fearing he might be dismissed. There was good reason for Thomas to worry about this; research assistants who had touted their accomplishments often paid a steep price for speaking out. A notable case involved Albert Schatz, a research assistant at Rutgers University in New Jersey. Schatz single-handedly isolated the bacterium that could stop the growth of tuberculosis and led to the creation of streptomycin, the first and only drug back then that could save the lives of millions of TB suffers. But it was the head of the laboratory, Dr. Selman Waxman, who received all the credit and rewards for the discovery, including a Nobel Prize and considerable financial gain. Schatz eventually sued over the slight and won — but he never again worked in a top-level microbiology lab.

In the end, the responsibility for Thomas's initial lack of recognition was Blalock's. Blalock was not just a respected and honored researcher; he was the head of both the surgical and research departments at Johns Hopkins and, after the blue baby operation, the most powerful surgeon in the world. He had worked for many years with Thomas, had seen him grow intellectually, and knew precisely what Thomas had contributed to his own success. Blalock could have pushed his talented research assistant's career forward with little trouble, and he could have fended off any criticism hurled at him. But he didn't. Instead, Blalock was, like too many people in positions of power, happy to allow an unfair situation to drift along, possibly hoping it would correct itself somehow, but not willing to create any problems that might unsettle his world. Dr. Bahnson sadly admitted, "The race issue was quite a concern, as you know, and Vivien was slow to get credit. He got a fair amount, but perhaps he should have gotten more credit earlier."

Dr. Levi Watkins, the first African American to be accepted at and to graduate from Vanderbilt's School of Medicine, became

Students in the last operative surgery class with Vivien Thomas (*background, right*) before the Hunterian Laboratory was torn down, 1955.

the first black chief resident of cardiac surgery at Johns Hopkins. He had worked closely with Thomas during the 1970s. For a very long time, Watkins felt that Thomas was "the most un-talked about, unappreciated, unknown giant in the African American community. What he helped facilitate impacted people all over the world."

Recognition did eventually begin to flow Thomas's way. In July 1951 — seven years after the first blue baby operation —

Thomas was always proud of the students he helped train. Among them was Dr. Levi Watkins, the first African American to graduate from Vanderbilt's School of Medicine and the first black chief resident of cardiac surgery at Johns Hopkins.

Dr. Raymond A. Heimbecker wrote a paper on his own blood circulation research and referred to Blalock and Thomas as co-contributors to the project (that is, they advised him on how to carry out his research and on what to test). "Heimbecker," Thomas reported with genuine surprise and delight, "thought my contribution to the project warranted the inclusion of my name. . . . This was the first paper on which my name appeared . . . with that of Alfred Blalock."

Blalock could have had Thomas's name removed from the paper, but he didn't. In fact, he felt it was a wonderful idea that Thomas's name be included. More recognition came to Thomas in the years to follow, including an honorary doctorate from Johns Hopkins. He would eventually be made head of the laboratory, responsible for teaching the surgical techniques he had perfected to new generations of young doctors, many of whom became world-famous heart surgeons.

One such student was Denton Cooley, who had participated in the first blue baby operation and became the first surgeon to successfully implant a completely artificial heart into a human. Cooley always admired Thomas and had great praise for his teacher's brilliant skills. "Even if you'd never seen surgery before," he told a reporter for *Washingtonian* magazine in 1989, "you could do it because Vivien made it look so simple. There wasn't a false move, not a wasted motion, when he operated."

Thomas received what was probably his biggest honor in 1971. A painting of him was commissioned by a Johns Hopkins group called the Old Hands Club, an association of former students who had gone on to highly successful careers. The painting was going to be done by Bob Gee and presented to Johns Hopkins with the understanding that it would hang in the laboratory where Thomas had created surgical techniques and tools and taught hundreds of students. On the day of the presentation, Thomas, in keeping with his shy nature, told his wife and family that something nice was going to happen to him that day, though he didn't say exactly what.

But this would be a moment when even Thomas was surprised. When the painting was presented to the president of

Portrait of Blalock by I. Hunter Parsons, 1945.

the hospital, Dr. Russell Nelson, he told the hundreds of guests

assembled, "Well, we are very honored to accept this." He then

turned to Thomas and with a smile added, "Vivien, I think you

should hang on the wall with all of your colleagues. You are go-

Portrait of Thomas by Bob Gee, 1969.

ing to be right there in the Blalock Building along with the other great Hopkins surgeons."

There was a momentary pause as everyone assembled on the lawn that day — surgeons Thomas had trained in years past, young students he was still training, nurses who had seen his surgical skills firsthand, even a number of janitors—took in what had been said. Then as one they stood to cheer the tall, humble man standing on the platform.

Even though he never operated on a human, his portrait hangs in the great hall of the Alfred Blalock Clinical Sciences Building, shoulder to shoulder with those of other internationally famous surgeons, including his friend, associate, and creative partner, Dr. Alfred Blalock.

Thomas had seen his dream of becoming a doctor evaporate because of a terrible economic collapse; he had been forced out of necessity to take a job that did not pay very well; he had been the target of discrimination and had been excluded from socializing with colleagues in public. Even so, he stayed true to the lessons he learned from his hard-working parents—he not only worked steadily and conscientiously day after day, year after year, but he did so with an eye to perfection. And doing this made him legendary.

Yet Thomas always remained perfectly grounded. He even managed to have a sense of humor about his portrait, saying, "It took quite some time for me to become accustomed to 'meeting myself' each morning in the Blalock lobby." He would then make his way to the laboratory, his sanctuary for over thirty years. As for his growing fame, Thomas took his usual practical approach,

After decades of standing in the background unnoticed, Vivien Thomas received his honorary Doctor of Laws degree in 1976.

one that stressed community involvement over his own ego. "As for me," he wrote in a letter to a colleague in 1975, "I just work here—I much prefer to leave [my place in medical history] to be expressed by you and others with whom I've worked. I've thoroughly enjoyed the role I have played and only tried to be me."

And by being himself, Vivien Thomas helped save thousands of lives and helped change the course of medicine forever.

A rare moment for Thomas, when he wasn't setting up an experiment, analyzing the results of an experiment, or teaching surgical techniques to students.

ACKNOWLEDGMENTS

I WANT to thank the following individuals and institutions for their generous help and encouragement: Dr. Michael A. Parziale of the Summit Medical Group for describing in detail what it is like to cut into a human chest and what a surgeon then encounters; Dr. Vincent P. Laudone of Memorial Sloan Kettering Cancer Center for describing the difficulties of performing intricate surgery in such a small, tight space as the human chest; Dr. Florence J. Grant of Memorial Sloan Kettering Cancer Center for discussing the difficulties involved in using the open drop technique to administer anesthesia; and archivists Jolie Braun of the Duke University Medical Archives, Ken Hoge of the Texas Heart Institute, and Timothy Wisniewski of the Alan Mason Chesney Medical Archives of the Johns Hopkins Medical Institutions for providing information and helping me to secure images.

SOURCE NOTES

Preface

xi Descriptions of operating room 706 and the tension of those taking part in the surgery are drawn from Thomas, 99–100, and Stoney, 68–69.

A description of Eileen Saxon's medical condition, plus details about the operation, can be found at www.neonatology.org/pdf/bluebabyoperation.pdf. Another interesting look at the operation can be found in Steve Catoe's blog, *Adventures of a Funky Heart!,* tricuspid.wordpress.com.

xi–xii "I took . . . die": Stoney, 68–69.

xii "Bill . . . days": Stoney, 68.

1. In the "Dog House"

1 Information about the Hunterian Laboratory and its shabby condition came from Thomas, 55–56 and 190–91, and Stoney, 162.

"drab hospital-green": Thomas, 55.

"[Dr. Blalock and I] . . . 'dog house'": Thomas, 55.

1–2 "Baltimore . . . fill them": Thomas, 57.

2–3 "individual dwellings . . . room": Thomas, 57.

Baltimore and prejudice are discussed passionately in Wilkerson, 8–11, 31, 37–45, 76–78, 398, and 408. Additional information came from Richard Paul Fuke, "Blacks, Whites, and Guns: Interracial Violence in Post-emancipation Maryland," *Maryland Historical Magazine* 92 (Fall 1997), 326–47, and Christopher Phillips, *Freedom's Port: The African American Community of Baltimore, 1790–1860* (Champaign: University of Illinois Press, 1997).

3 "There was . . . anyplace else": C. Fraser Smith, quoted in *Partners of the Heart,* Act II.

4 "congested . . . grassless": Thomas, 57.

"Many . . . suitable": Thomas, 57.

6 "I would . . . challenge": Thomas, 56.

7 "I did . . . told": Thomas, 59.

7–8 "Who the hell . . . give it to him": Thomas, 60.

9 "frightening . . . person": Arthur F. Raper, *The Tragedy of Lynching* (Chapel Hill: University of North Carolina Press, 1933), 36–37.

"In everyday . . . brutal": Wilkerson, 42.

10 "Dr. Blalock . . . of him": Thomas, 16.

"I told . . . the hall": Thomas, 16.

10–11 Several works were consulted for Alfred Blalock's early history, including A. McGehee Harvey, *Alfred Blalock: 1899–1964* (Washington, D.C., National Academy of Sciences, 1982), 49–52; H. William Scott, *History of Surgery at Vanderbilt University* (Nashville: Vanderbilt University Medical Center,

1996), 52–58; and Mark M. Ravitch, *The Papers of Alfred Blalock,* vol. I (Baltimore: Johns Hopkins Press, 1966), xv–xxi.

11   "apologized . . . to work": Thomas, 16.

"We had . . . mistakes": Thomas, 17.

11–12   "The day . . . other": Thomas, 60.

12   "[Johns] Hopkins . . . fortress": C. Fraser Smith, *Partners of the Heart,* Act II.

13   "Trash cans . . . dusted": Thomas, 62.

"was . . . too": Thomas, 62.

"Knowing . . . situation": Thomas, 63.

"no intention . . . here": Thomas, 63.

"Good Lord . . . already": Thomas, 62.

"I answered . . . later": Thomas, 62–63.

14   "had . . . happen": Thomas, 63.

2. The Professor and His Assistant

16–17   A concise description of Blalock's and Thomas's work on shock at Vanderbilt is in Harvey, 52–56. Thomas details this work as well, 14, 21–26, 33, 38, 66–68, and 75–77.

The various forms of shock and their symptoms are discussed by Eugene A. Stead in "Circulatory Collapse and Shock," *Textbook of Medicine,* vol. I (Philadelphia: W. B. Saunders, 1967), 587–90.

18   "I want . . . can't do": Thomas, 10.

19   "I want . . . around": Thomas, 10–11.

"To me . . . months": Thomas, 11.

Thomas and Blalock had a long history regarding Thomas's salary, documented in Thomas, 11, 18–19, 44, 65–66, and

181–82. Before the surge in medical research after the blue baby operation, no one at a research laboratory made a great deal of money, not even the director. In addition to being African American, Thomas had two major obstacles to overcome in order to earn a fair salary. First, he had come to Vanderbilt as an unskilled janitor and was paid accordingly. Second, he sought employment at the beginning of the Great Depression, when millions of people were losing their jobs. Business owners felt that anyone working for them was lucky to be earning a regular income and weren't very generous with starting salaries or subsequent annual raises.

Thomas grumbled about his wages frequently, and Blalock grumbled about his assistant's frequent requests and occasional threats to resign over his low salary. Blalock had to get permission from senior administrators in the university to increase Thomas's wages, which he eventually always did. Thomas always felt his contributions to Blalock's research should result in a higher salary, but he never suggested that Blalock was taking advantage of him because he was African American.

Background information on Thomas and his upbringing is from Thomas, 3–8.

"Our parents . . . expectations": Thomas, 5.

"excellent seamstress": Thomas, 4.

20 "My father . . . carpentry": Thomas, 6.

"So we . . . Saturdays": Thomas, 6.

"I . . . embarrass you": Thomas, 7.

21 "my father . . . old": Thomas, 6.

22–23 Blalock and a fellow doctor, J. W. Beard, described their very careful research methods in two journal articles: *Archives of Surgery* 22, no. 617 (April 1931), and the *Journal of Clinical Investigations* 11, no. 311 (March 1932). Thomas elaborated on Blalock's research techniques and his training in Thomas, 23–29.

23 "Dr. Blalock . . . conclusions": Thomas, 27.

24 "The volume . . . being done": Thomas, 24.

25 "I did . . . activity": Thomas, 25.

3. Surrounded by Failure

27–29 A more visual presentation of fetal heart development can be found on the U.S. National Library of Medicine site: www.ncbi.nlm.mik.gov/pmc/articles/PMC1767109.

28 Dr. Mark Hill of the University of South Wales provided a clear description of fetal heart development. He has also created a website on the subject: embryology.med.unsw.edu.au/embryology/index.php?title=Basic_Cardiac_Embryology. "Congenital . . . size": G. Wayne Miller, *King of Hearts: The True Story of the Maverick Who Pioneered Open Heart Surgery* (New York: Crown, 2000), 115–16.

28–29 A technical study of congenital heart defects, with detailed illustrations, is found in Allen D. Everett and D. Scott Lim, *Illustrated Field Guide to Congenital Heart Disease and Repair* (Charlottesville, Va.: Scientific Software Solutions, 2010), 92–95.

29–32 A very good discussion of Helen Taussig's family, upbringing, and early education can be found in Baldwin, 3–17.

30–31 In 1969 only 9 percent of all medical students were women. A year later, the Women's Action Group filed a class action suit against every medical teaching facility in the United States, claiming discrimination in their admission policies. Medical schools immediately began to admit more women, and today more than 50 percent of all medical students are women. A very clear overview of this situation can be found in Walsh. Learn more about Taussig's personal struggle to become a doctor in Baldwin, 22–28.

30 "My father . . . undertook": Baldwin, 14.

31 "so . . . students": Baldwin, 24.

32 Many writers have described Taussig's loss of hearing and how she coped with it. Baldwin's account, 37–40, is concise and detailed.

33 "Adversity . . . with her": Baldwin, 17, 40.

33–34 Tetralogy of Fallot was described as long ago as 1672 by the Catholic bishop and scientist Niels Stensen, who did pioneering research in both anatomy and geology, and was eventually named for the French physician Étienne-Louis Arthur Fallot. The condition currently occurs in approximately 400 babies per 1 million births (or 52,000 per year worldwide). It is very treatable, especially when diagnosed and treated early. World and Olympic snowboarding champion Shaun White was operated on for the defect twice before his first birthday.

A clinical explanation of the defect is found in Beeson and McDermott, 612. Also see Stoney, 8; Thomas, 80–81; and Weisse, 40–41. Two reliable websites also provide information and illustrations. One is at the National Heart, Lung, and Blood Institute (www.nhlbi.nih.gov/health/health-topics/topics/tof) and the other is at the Centers for Disease Control and Prevention (www.cdc.gov/ncbddd/heartdefects/TetralogyOfFallot.html).

35 "You . . . make one": Stoney, 200.

"It seemed . . . time": Baldwin, 52.

35–36 "When . . . chance": Baldwin, 52.

4. Answered and Unanswered Questions

37–38 "The perception . . . cases": Jody Bart, ed., *Women Succeeding in the Sciences: Theories and Practices Across Disciplines* (West Lafayette, Ind.: Purdue University Press, 2000), 4. Taussig and Blalock had an interesting working relationship, to say the least. Both were experts in their fields; both had strong egos and were not afraid to express their opinions. And both made decisions for their desperately ill young patients that literally could mean life or death. No wonder they became tense and snappy at times. For additional details about how they worked together, see Stoney, 11–12, 68, 165–66, 246, and 261–63.

Thomas was in many ways an enigmatic person. He wrote what some people refer to as an autobiography, but most of it is about the work and people he was involved with. An interesting note is that many doctors and nurses had opinions about both Taussig and Blalock and were sometimes a bit critical. Apparently no one has, or had, a bad word to say about Thomas, which speaks highly of his skills and personality. A number of doctors discuss Thomas in Stoney, 167, 185, 191, 223, and 246–47.

38   "Dr. Taussig . . . care": Stoney, 165.

    "Dr. Taussig . . . so much": Stoney, 115.

39   "a pleasant personality": Thomas, 80.

40   "She expressed . . . around": Thomas, 80–81.

    For how Blalock and Thomas came to do the research on tetralogy of Fallot, see Stoney, 67–68; Thomas, 77 and 80–81; and Weisse, 42–43.

40–41   "sure . . . tested": Thomas, 82.

41   "I spent . . . specimens": Thomas, 81.

    "amazed . . . at all": Thomas, 81.

    "If . . . helplessness": Thomas, 81.

42–45   It would require many hundreds of pages to describe the use of animals in biomedical research, its history and abuses, the slowly changing attitudes about it in the medical community and the public, and how animal rights protesters, computers, and the use of cells for research have reduced the number of animals being used for experimentation. To keep my discussion concise, I focused on the state of animal research around the time when the blue baby operation was being perfected.

    One of Vivien Thomas's responsibilities was caring for the animals used in research at Johns Hopkins, and he did an especially fine job. He felt, as might be expected, that use of animal subjects was crucial to his and Dr. Blalock's research, and he discusses this in Thomas, 152–53. He also talks about an ongoing program at Johns Hopkins that had all surgeons, from Blalock to the newest resident, set aside Friday afternoons for a veterinary clinic where local pets were treated and sometimes operated on for various conditions. See Thomas, 207–9.

The following short list of books will provide a good, solid background in the history of biomedical research and animal rights:

Cunningham, Andrew. *The Laboratory Revolution in Medicine.* Cambridge: Cambridge University Press, 1992.

Jasper, James, and Dorothy Nelkin. *The Animal Rights Crusade: The Growth of Moral Protest.* New York: The Free Press, 1992.

National Research Council. *Use of Laboratory Animals in Biomedical and Behavioral Research.* Washington, D.C.: National Academy Press, 1988.

Rollin, Bernard E., and M. Lynne Kesel, *The Experimental Animal in Biomedical Research: A Survey of Scientific and Ethical Issues for Investigators,* vol. 1. Boca Raton, Fla.: CRC Press, 1990.

Turner, James. *Reckoning with the Beast: Animals, Pain and Humanity in the Victorian Mind.* Baltimore: Johns Hopkins University Press, 1995.

The following websites provide general information about animal rights and the use of animals in biomedical research:

American Association for Laboratory Animal Science: www.aalas.org

American Society for the Prevention of Cruelty to Animals: www.aspca.org

The Humane Society of the United States:

www.humanesociety.org

People for the Ethical Treatment of Animals: www:peta.org

44 "The dog . . . ideal": Stoney, 93.

"Without . . . nowhere": Miller, 67.

"I know . . . of ways": Miller, 73.

"clinical . . . therapy": Shumacker, 41.

45 An amazing aspect of the history of cardiac surgery is how very little history there was before the first blue baby operation in 1944. A concise look at pre–blue baby cardiac surgery can be found in Shumacker, 1–40. Also see Stoney, 1–7, 129, and 197.

5. The Search

51 "something the Lord had made": Thomas, 122.

It was not unusual for surgeons and their laboratory assistants to create surgical tools for a particular operation. Often these new tools were improvements on existing tools, which was the case when Thomas and Longmire designed the adjustable clamp that became known as the Blalock clamp. After they had drawn up a design, Thomas took their drawings to a nearby tool-making company, where the new clamp was produced. Back when the blue baby operation was introduced, most of the designers of such tools did not receive any payment. The companies that made the tools would provide the inventors with free instruments and sell the instruments to other surgeons. Today everyone involved (the designers, medical schools, and manufacturers) shares in the profits. Thomas discusses the creation of the Blalock clamp in Thomas, 96.

53   "It is . . . solved": R. B. Pond, quoted in Thomas, 89.

54   "As Dr. Taussig . . . where": Thomas, 89.

6. "All the World Is Against It"

55   "brain power . . . projects": Thomas, 178.

"He was . . . the time": Stoney, 245.

Many surgeons who worked with Blalock commented on his abilities as a surgeon. Some viewed him as solid but not inspired. Others felt he was a fine surgeon who could handle even the most difficult surgical situations. For a variety of comments on Blalock's surgical skills, see Stoney, 69–70, 115, 117, 164, 180, 186–87, 245, 258, and 260.

56   "was very . . . technician": Stoney, 260.

60–61   It appears that after the success of the first blue baby operation, Dr. Austin Lamont did administer anesthesia to very young patients. A very nice tribute to Lamont, "Austin Lamont and the Evolution of Modern Academic American Anesthesiology," by Stanley Mursvchick, M.D., and Henry Rosenberg, M.D., appeared in the *Journal of the American Society of Anesthesiologists* 84, no. 2 (February 1996): 436–91.

61   "When suffering . . . burden": Peter Safer, "Tribute to Dr. Austin Lamont," *Anesthesiology* 87, no. 2 (August 1997): 461.

"Surgery . . . of the heart": Stephen Paget, *Surgery of the Chest* (London: John Wright, 1896), 121.

61–62 "The heart . . . techniques": Mike Field, "I Remember . . .
Thinking It Was Impossible," *The Gazette: The Newspaper
of Johns Hopkins University,* May 30, 1995, 8.

64 "This was . . . available": Stoney, 12.
"Many of us . . . disaster": Stoney, 245.

65 "You know . . . right": Weisse, 77.

7. "Vivien, You'd Better Come Down Here"

66 "had said . . . nervous": Thomas, 92.

67 "Miss Puryear . . . down here": Thomas, 92.

68 "The patient . . . drapes": Thomas, 92.

68–70 There have been numerous descriptions of the first blue baby
operation, with Blalock's own postoperative notes the most
direct. Thomas describes it in detail in Thomas, 91–95.
Several other descriptions appear in Stoney, 8–14, 68–70,
115–66, and 244–45.

69–70 "less than . . . procedure": Thomas, 93.

70 "Dr. Blalock . . . to him": Stoney, 244.

70–71 "I watched . . . direction": Thomas, 95.

71 "was . . . there": Stoney, 69.
"disturbed . . . thrill": Blalock's surgical notes, from the Alan
Mason Chesney Medical Archives of the Johns Hopkins
Medical Institutions.
"The color is improving" and "Take a look": Stoney, 70.
When Eileen Saxon's operation was complete, Merel Harmel
noted that her blue skin was "improving"—that is, becoming
less blue—and that her change in color was "quite dramatic."
Neither Blalock, Thomas, nor Taussig ever contradicted these

descriptions, though it is interesting that these three were always very matter-of-fact about Eileen's skin color change. Blalock always said the immediate color change was evident but never described it as dramatic, and Thomas never mentioned it at all. Harmel is quoted in Stoney, 70. It is my opinion that some of the more dramatic descriptions that have appeared over the years in articles and movies were actually describing later operations on older children, where increased oxygen had an instant and obvious effect on skin color.

72–73 "leaned over . . . dramatic": Stoney, 70.

8. Then What Happened?

75–76 "because . . . monitoring": Stoney, 143.

Surgery and postoperative care were both in their infancy in the mid-1940s. Operating rooms were not completely sterile areas. It was not unusual, for instance, for a doctor to come in from the street and go directly into the room where an operation was in progress to chat with a fellow surgeon. Pieces of equipment such as lamps and chairs were often brought into were operating rooms without being sterilized.

Postoperative care was primitive, to say the least. A doctor or nurse would simply look in on patients to make sure they were doing okay; there were no electronic monitors to check heart rate, for instance. A discussion of what surgery and aftercare were like can be found in Stoney, xi–xii, 12–13, 69, 101, 197–98, 245–46, and 514. Also see Shumacker, 42–43.

76 "Eileen's . . . pink": Thomas, 95–96.

Almost nothing is known about Eileen Saxon or her family. All written sources about her sound identical and seem to have been drawn from information gathered when she was admitted to Johns Hopkins in 1944. It appears that the family was poor and that her operation and stay in the hospital were free, which means no information (such as her parents' names and address) was gathered for billing purposes.

We know that the first blue baby operation improved her health and that she was discharged after a lengthy stay at Johns Hopkins. Then, several months later, she began suffering blue baby symptoms again and had a second operation, this time on the opposite side of her chest. She survived the operation, but died several days later, just short of her third birthday.

77 "Some . . . patients": Thomas, 97.

78 "To these . . . praying for": Thomas, 97.

Blalock became one of the world's first superstar surgeons after the blue baby operation. His fame embarrassed him, since it was generally considered unethical for surgeons to promote themselves in newspapers and magazine articles. For more information on the importance of the operation and Blalock's international fame, see Stoney, 14–18, 70–71, 186, 237, 247–48, and 264. Also see Shumacker, 66 and 69–70.

"literally . . . start": Stoney, 16.

79 "a forceful and impressive presentation": Stoney, 15.

79–80 "A long . . . earlier": Stoney, 15–16.

80 "There was . . . breakthrough": Stoney, 264.

80–81 Alfred Blalock had one of the most successful research and
teaching careers in the history of medicine. He became
internationally famous for his studies and publications on
shock, then became even more famous with his blue baby
operation. Both of these innovations saved hundreds of
thousands of lives and changed medical history. He would
eventually write more than two hundred articles plus a book
(*Principles of Surgery, Shock and Other Problems*), receive nine
honorary degrees from research universities, be a member of
forty-three medical societies, and be given numerous awards
for his medical research, including the Passano Award, the
Matas Award, and the Albert Lasker Medical Research Award,
as well as France's highest award for public service, Chevalier
de la Légion d'Honneur. He died of cancer in 1964, shortly
after he retired from Johns Hopkins.

81 "more than . . . era": Stoney, 18.

84 Jamie Wyeth was just seventeen years old when he painted
Taussig's portrait. The painting was considered so offensive
that Taussig wrapped it in a bath towel and stored it away
in a spare room in her house for years. After her death, it
was donated to Johns Hopkins, but it never hung in the hall
where Blalock's and Thomas's portraits are displayed. It
ended up in a little-used room, but was later removed
when doctors who knew and had worked with Taussig
complained. It now hangs in a private office at Johns
Hopkins. In his defense, Wyeth said he was struck by
Taussig's intensity and wanted to capture that on canvas.
"I felt I had caught something, not that it was something

cruel, not that it was something ugly, but I had really
caught the personality of this person as I saw her" (quoted
in Patricia Mersal, "The Changing Face of a Strong Woman,"
www.newyorktimes.com/2013/08/18/arts/design/
a-showing-for-3). Two paintings of Taussig were
commissioned later; they are pleasant, accurate portrayals,
but both are bland and lifeless. Wyeth created a genuine
work of art that did not reflect what Taussig's friends and
colleagues saw in her.

84–85 "Physician . . . heart": Baldwin, 111.

85–86 The exact nature of Taussig's role in developing the original
blue baby procedure has been argued for years. A few say that
during the first meeting with Blalock and Thomas, she
suggested the specific procedure that could bring more
oxygenated blood to a patient's heart; according to others,
she simply wondered if this might be possible surgically.
It's important to remember that Taussig never claimed to
have suggested the research path that should be taken; nor
did Blalock, who gave his colleague great credit for the
operation. Thomas says she explained genetic cardiac defects
in great detail and wondered if it might be possible to "redo
the plumbing" of a child's body to allow more oxygenated
blood to circulate. I assume she mentioned Dr. Gross's
procedure because that is what took her up to Boston to talk
with him. For a variety of opinions on this, see Stoney, 9, 12,
14, 70, 115, 159, 166, 186, and 245–46. Also see Weisse, 43
and 380–81; Baldwin, 52; and Thomas, 80–81.

86 "led to . . . paper": Blalock and Taussig, 189–202.

89 "to . . . his own": Thomas, 10–11.

90 "Dr. Blalock . . . Blalock": Stoney, 191.

91 "Vivien was not . . . imagination": Dr. Levi Watkins Jr., quoted in *Partners of the Heart*, Act III.

"I think the gentlemen . . . time": Dr. Levi Watkins Jr., quoted in *Partners of the Heart*, Act III.

92 "The race issue . . . earlier": Stoney, 191.

93 "the most . . . world": Dr. Levi Watkins Jr., quoted in *Partners of the Heart*, Act I.

94 "Heimbecker thought . . . Alfred Blalock": Thomas, 152.

95 "Even if you'd never seen . . . operated": *Washingtonian* magazine, August 1989, 110.

96–97 "Well, we . . . surgeons": Stoney, 265.

98 "It took quite some time . . . lobby": Thomas, 221.

Following Blalock's death, Vivien Thomas sank into a depression for several years, during which he did very little research work. Eventually he resumed his research and remained the supervisor of the surgical laboratory at Johns Hopkins until 1985, for a total of thirty-five years. After receiving his honorary doctorate, he was named an instructor of surgery at the school, an extraordinarily rare appointment for someone who was neither a surgeon nor a doctor. He died of pancreatic cancer in 1985.

By this time, everyone at Johns Hopkins knew about Thomas's genius for research and his remarkable surgical skills; many other surgeons in the United States also knew about him. The world learned about him posthumously in August 1989, when Katie McCabe published her National

Magazine Award–winning article, "Like Something the Lord Made," in *Washingtonian* magazine. Over the years, additional honors came Thomas's way: the Congressional Black Caucus Foundation set up the Vivien Thomas Scholarship for Medical Science and Research; the *Journal of Surgical Case Reports* named its annual award for best-written case report for Thomas; and the Baltimore City Public School System opened the Vivien T. Thomas Medical Arts Academy, a high school with a focus on the health professions, mathematics, and sciences.

Both Vivien Thomas and Alfred Blalock prided themselves on the medical students they trained and sent out into the world. Many of these individuals became world famous and innovative surgeons, with more than twenty of them heading up cardiac departments in hospitals throughout the United States. Thomas was especially proud of welcoming and mentoring a succession of African American students, one of whom was his nephew Koco Eaton.

99 "As for me . . . to be me": Thomas, 219–20.

BIBLIOGRAPHY

Baldwin, Joyce. *To Heal the Heart of a Child: Helen Taussig, M.D.* New York: Walker and Company, 1992.

Beeson, Paul B., and Walsh McDermott. *Textbook of Medicine.* Philadelphia: W. B. Saunders Company, 1967.

Blalock, Alfred, and Helen B. Taussig. "The Surgical Treatment of Malformations of the Heart in Which There Is Pulmonary Stenosis or Atresia." *Journal of the American Medical Association* 128 (1945): 189–202.

Comroe, Julius H. *Exploring the Heart: Discoveries in Heart Disease and High Blood Pressure.* New York: W. W. Norton & Company, 1983.

Gilbert, Lynn, and Gaylan Moore. *Particular Passions: Talks with Women Who Have Shaped Our Times.* New York: Clarkson N. Potter, 1981.

Harvey, W. Proctor. "A Conversation with Helen Taussig." *Medical Times* 106, no. 11 (1978): 28–44.

McNamara, Dan G., ed. "Helen Brooke Taussig: 1898 to 1986." *Journal of the American College of Cardiology* 10, no. 3 (1987): 662–66.

Partners of the Heart. PBS documentary, transcript. www.pbs.org/wgbh/amex/partners/filmmore/pt.html.

Ravitch, M. M. *The Papers of Alfred Blalock*. Baltimore: Johns Hopkins Press, 1966.

Schwertly-McNamara, Cathy. *Memoirs of a Blue Baby*. Bloomington, Ind.: Xlibras, 2010.

Shumacker, Harris B. *The Evolution of Cardiac Surgery*. Bloomington: Indiana University Press, 1992.

Stoney, William S. *Pioneers of Cardiac Surgery*. Nashville: Vanderbilt University Press, 2008.

Taussig, Helen B. *Congenital Malformations of the Heart*. New York: Commonwealth Fund, 1947.

Thomas, Vivien T. *Partners of the Heart*. Philadelphia: University of Pennsylvania Press, 1985.

Walsh, Mart Roth. *Doctors Wanted: No Women Need Apply: Sexual Barriers in the Medical Profession, 1835–1975*. New Haven, Conn.: Yale University Press, 1977.

Weisse, Allen B. *Heart to Heart: The Twentieth Century Battle Against Cardiac Disease*. New Brunswick, N.J.: Rutgers University Press, 2002.

Wilkerson, Isabel. *The Warmth of Other Suns: The Epic Story of America's Great Migration*. New York: Random House, 2010.

PICTURE CREDITS

Alan Mason Chesney Medical Archives of the Johns Hopkins
    Medical Institutions: 5, 6, 18, 31, 34 (bottom), 36, 39, 46, 52,
    56, 69, 72–73, 77, 79, 84, 85, 88, 90, 93, 94, 96, 97, 99

Author's collection: 83

Bettmann/Corbis: 67, 80

Duke University Medical Archives: 17, 23, 62, 87

Estate of Yosef Karsh: 12, 82

Hulton Archive/Getty Images: 43

Leon Schlossberg drawing/*JAMA*: 49

Library of Congress: 4, 21

Morton Tadder/Baltimore: 33

National Library of Medicine: 34 (top), 64

New Contributed Photographs Collection, Otis Historical Archives,
    National Museum of Health and Medicine: 24

Oklahoma Historical Society: 9

Texas Heart Institute, www.texasheart.org: 59

With permission of the Thomas family: 2

INDEX

Page numbers in **bold** refer to photos and illustrations.

anesthesia, xii, 22, 60–61, 63, 67, **67,** 68, 113

animal rights, 42, **43,** 45

animals, experimental
    Anna (dog), 88, **88**
    at Johns Hopkins, 1, 22, 42, 45, **46,** 110–11
    overview, 42–44, 45, 110
    in tetralogy of Fallot research, 47–54, 58, 69–70

antibacterials, 74, 75, 91–92

Baltimore, MD, 1–4, **4**

Begg, Dr. Alexander, 32

birth defects
    heart, 29, 33–34, 41 (*See also* tetralogy of Fallot)
    from thalidomide, 84

Blalock, Dr. Alfred, **12, 17, 79, 80**
    background, 10–11, 56–57
    confidence issues, xii–xiii, 55, 58, 59, 64, 66–67
    death, 119
    description, 13
    education, 56–57
    first meeting with Taussig, 37, 39–40, 117–18
    notoriety, 76–80, **77, 82,** 82–83, 116, 118–19
    other blue baby surgeries, 76, 81, **82,** 82–83, 86
    personality, 10, 78, 80
    portrait, **96**
    relationship with Taussig, 38, 85–86, 109
    relationship with Thomas,

Blalock, Dr. Alfred (*cont.*)
  relationship with Thomas,
    xiii, 10 11, 14 15, 55,
    58, 70–71, 86–92
  reputation, 16, 36, 57, 80–
    81, 82, 113
  Saxon's surgery, xi–xiii, 63,
    66–74, **72–73**
  Saxon's treatment, 58–60,
    62, 64–65
  shock research, 16–17, **24,**
    25–26, 40, 81
  as a teacher, 17, **18,** 120
  tetralogy of Fallot research,
    40–41, 45–54, 55, 86
  at Vanderbilt, 17, **23,** 53, 57
  See also Hunterian
    Laboratory
blood
  oxygenation, 27, 34, 40, 47–
    50, 53, 72–73, 114–15
  whole blood or plasma, **24,**
    25
blue baby syndrome. *See*
    tetralogy of Fallot

Children's Cardiac Clinic, xii,
    29, 32, 37–38, **39,** 64, 84
clamp, Blalock, 51, **52,** 112
Cooley, Dr. Denton A., 38, 55,
    59, 60, 64, 70, 95

Davis, Jefferson, 10
ductus arteriosus, patent, 34–35

Eaton, Koco, 120

Fallot, Étienne-Louis Arthur,
    34, **34,** 108

Great Depression, **21,** 22, 106
Gross, Dr. Robert E., 34, **34,** 35,
    39, 44, 118

Haller, Dr. J. Alex, Jr., 55–56, **56,**
    80
Harmel, Dr. Merel, 62–63, 68,
    71, 114–15
Harrison, Tinsley, 56–57
heart, dog, 48–50, 69–70
heart, human
  anatomy, 27, **49**
  congenital disease, 29, 33–
    34, 41 (*See also* tetralogy
    of Fallot)
  development, 27–29, **28,** 34
  modern inventions to treat,
    44, 45, 75–76, 81, 115
  in pathology museum, 29,
    41, 45
heart surgery
  on an infant, **49,** 50, **69**
  artificial heart, 61, 81, 95

heart transplant, 61, 95

history of, 61–62, 115

open-heart, 44

on Saxon, xi–xiii, 63, 66–74, **72–73**

tools and supplies, 45, 48–51, **52,** 63, 68–69, **69,** 81–83, 112–13

Heimbecker, Dr. Raymond A., 94

Hunterian Laboratory

"Dog House," 1, **5**

experimental animals, 1, 42, 45, 110–11

housekeeper issues, 13–14

poor condition of, 1, 4–7, **6**

surgery class, **93**

hypertension, 35, 40, 53

Johns Hopkins Hospital

notoriety, 76–77, **77,** 81, 82–83

Saxson's surgery, xi–xiii, 63, 66–74, **72–73**

surgical house staff, **79**

veterinary clinic, 111

Watkins at, 93, 94

See also Children's Cardiac Clinic

Johns Hopkins University School of Medicine

Blalock's responsibilities, 8, 14, 57–58, 62, **62,** 63, 92

notoriety, 81

rejection of Blalock, 57

salary issues, 106

Taussig as student, 32

See also Hunterian Laboratory

Johnson, Lyndon B., 84–85, **85**

Johnson & Johnson, 51, **83**

Lamont, Dr. Austin, xii, 60–61, 62, 113

Lillehei, Dr. C. Walton, 43–44

Longmire, Dr. William, **64**

and Saxon, xi–xiii, 60, 64, 71, 72, 73

surgical tool development, 51, 112

lungs, 49–50

media attention, 76–78, **77,** 116

Mitchell, Charlotte, 60

needles, suturing, 51, 63

Nelson, Dr. Russell, 96–97

oxygen

blood oxygenation, 27, 34, 40, 47–50, 53, 72–73, 114–15

oxygen (*cont.*)

    supply to the fetus, 28

    tent to administer, 58

    used during surgery, 63

Paget, Dr. Stephen, 61

post-operative care, 75–76, 115

Poth, Dr. Edgar, 7–8, 11, 13–14

prejudice. *See* racial

    discrimination; sex

    discrimination

Puryear, Clara Belle, 67

racial discrimination

    Jim Crow laws, 3–4, **4,** 10,

        14

    against Thomas, xiii, 3–4, 7,

        10–15, 91–93, 98, 106

    violence in the South, 8–9, **9**

Saxon, Eileen

    background, 116

    condition, 58, 63, 65, 76,

        114–15

    death, 116

    notoriety, 76–78, **77**

    post-surgery, 75–76

    surgery, xi–xiii, 63, 66–74,

        72–73

    treatment, 58–60, 62–65

Schatz, Albert, 91–92

scientific creativity, 53

scientific credit, 91–92

sex discrimination, 31, 108

Sherwood, Elizabeth, 63

shock, 16–17, **24,** 25–26, 40, 42,

    119

Stensen, Niels, 108

sterile environment, 115

Taussig, Dr. Helen, **36, 80**

    background, 29–30

    description, 29

    education, 30–32

    first meeting with Blalock,

        37, 39–40, 117–18

    head of Children's Cardiac

        Clinic, xii, 29, 32, 37–38,

        84

    heart defects research, 29,

        35, 40, 41, 83–84, **87,**

        117–18

    notoriety, 78–79, 83–86, **85**

    portraits, **84,** 117

    relationship with Blalock,

        38, 51, 85–86, 109

    and Saxon, 58–60, 63–64,

        71, 72

    treatment style, 32–33, **33,**

        37–38, **39,** 41

Taussig, Frank William (father),

    29–30, **31**

tetralogy of Fallot (blue baby syndrome)
  first description, 108
  incidence rate, 108
  medical lectures on, 78–80
  mortality rate, 34
  overview, 33–34
  research by Thomas and Blalock, 40–42, 45–54, 55, 58, 86
  surgeries, 76, **77,** 81–83, **82, 86, 87** (*See also* Saxon, Eileen)
  and Taussig, 35, 40–41, 117–18
thalidomide, 84
Thomas, Clara (wife), **2**
Thomas, Mary (mother), 19
Thomas, Vivien, **90, 100**
  background, 19–22, 89, 98
  and Blalock's death, 119
  description, 5, 10, 98
  education and degrees, 21–22, 94, **99**
  family, **2**
  first meeting with Taussig, 37, 39–40
  notoriety, 94–99, 119–20
  other blue baby surgeries, 76, 81, 82–83, 86, **87**
  personality, 19, 86, 98, 110
  portrait, 95–98, **97**
  and Poth, 7–8, 11–12
  racial discrimination against, xiii, 3–4, 7, 10–15, 91–93, 98, 106
  relationship with Blalock, xiii, 10–11, 14–15, 55, 58, 70–71, 76, 86–92
  research assist. at Johns Hopkins, 1–2, 4–8, 10–15, 25, 40–42, 45–56, **46,** 68, 86–92, 106
  research assist. at Vanderbilt, 10, 17–19, 22–25, **23,** 53
  and Saxon, xiii, 60, 63, 66–71
  surgical skills, **46,** 50–51, 89–90, **93,** 94–95, 119
  surgical tool development, 51, **52,** 63, 81–82, 112
  as a teacher, **93,** 95, 120
  work ethic, 19, 20, 98
Thomas, William (father), 19
tuberculosis, 30, 57, 91–92

Vanderbilt University, 6, 10, 16–19, 22–25, **23,** 53, 57, 92

Watkins, Dr. Levi, Jr., 91–93, **94**

Waxman, Dr. Selman, 92
White, Shaun, 108
World War II, 1, **24,** 25, **67**
Wyeth, Jamie, **84,** 117